Internet for English Teaching

Mark Warschauer, Heidi Shetzer, and Christine Meloni

TESOL

Founded 1966 Teachers of English to Speakers of Other Languages, Inc.

Typeset in Adobe Garamond and Belwe
by Capitol Communication Systems, Inc., Crofton, Maryland USA
and printed by
Pantagraph Printing, Bloomington, Illinois USA

Teachers of English to Speakers of Other Languages, Inc.
700 South Washington Street, Suite 200
Alexandria, Virginia 22314 USA
Tel. 703-836-0774 • Fax 703-836-7864 • E-mail tesol@tesol.org • http://www.tesol.org/

Director of Communications and Marketing: Helen Kornblum
Managing Editor: Marilyn Kupetz
Copy Editor: Ellen Garshick
Cover Design: Charles Akins

ISBN 0-939791-88-9
Library of Congress Catalogue No. 00-131612

Dedication

This book is dedicated to the memory of Roy Bowers, a colleague who helped us learn that the Internet is not about bytes and bits but about new possibilities of human connection and creativity.

Contents

Preface

In 1995, I authored *E-Mail for English Teaching*, the first major book about the uses of the Internet for English teachers and learners. *E-Mail for English Teaching* became one of TESOL's best-selling titles, won an international award from Educational Testing Service, and was translated into and published in Chinese and Japanese. I have savored the many e-mail messages I've received from teachers throughout the world sharing with me the impact the book has had on them and their students.

Five years, however, is a millennium as far as information technology goes. Since 1995, the Internet has grown from a resource accessible to a relatively small number of well-to-do users in certain industrialized countries to a mass medium of communication among hundreds of millions of people around the globe. At the same time, the nature of the Internet has changed as a result of the introduction of more sophisticated means of finding information and publishing on the World Wide Web. Meanwhile, the English teaching profession has continued to grow and change, with more emphasis placed than ever before on the development of skills for purposeful communication, critical literacy, and autonomous lifelong learning.

Because of all these changes, I have invited Heidi Shetzer and Christine Meloni, two international leaders in the field of on-line language learning, to join me in writing this book. *Internet for English Teaching* incorporates all we have learned about on-line education, including up-to-date information about multiclass on-line projects, multimedia authoring, distance education, and networking for professional development.

Who is *Internet for English Teaching* for? It is for you if

- You have been using the Internet in your teaching for years and want to read about the latest developments in research, theory, and curriculum.

- You have recently begun using the Internet in teaching and want to expand your repertoire of ideas, projects, and activities.
- You haven't used the Internet yet for teaching but are interested in an introduction to this field.

In short, we've combined pedagogical suggestions, research, and theory in a book that has something to offer educators from a variety of backgrounds.

We invite you to share your responses, ideas, thoughts, and suggestions with us by e-mail. Our communication with teachers around the world has allowed us to provide in this book a comprehensive overview of outstanding ways of using the Internet for English teaching. By sharing your comments and experiences, you can contribute to the creative collaboration that is at the heart of the best uses of the Internet.

Mark Warschauer
http://www.lll.hawaii.edu/markw
markw@hawaii.edu
American-Mideast Education and Training Services
(AMIDEAST)

Joined by
Heidi Shetzer
http://www.newtierra.com
heidi@newtierra.com
University of California, Santa Barbara, International Programs

Christine Meloni
http://gwis2.circ.gwu.edu/~meloni
meloni@gwu.edu
The George Washington University, Department of English
as a Foreign Language

Acknowledgments

The process of writing this book has been a testament to the value of Internet-based collaboration. We have sent and received tens of thousands of e-mail messages since 1995, corresponding with hundreds of colleagues around the world. We have learned from thousands of ESL and EFL educators who exchange thoughts and comments via personal e-mail, e-mail discussion lists, and the World Wide Web. The people whose ideas have inspired this book are far too numerous to name, and we apologize for not being able to acknowledge everyone individually. We have done our best to credit anyone whose specific words or materials we have used, and we apologize in advance if we have failed to do so. Please notify us if this is the case so that we can correct the matter in future printings.

We owe special thanks, though, to the following people. The editors and reviewers from TESOL have given us a great deal of guidance and advice, and we thank them for their professional wisdom. Our employers at AMIDEAST; the University of California, Santa Barbara; and The George Washington University have been fully supportive of our research on Internet-based learning, and we thank and congratulate them for their leadership in this important new educational area. And most of all, we thank our family members: Mark's wife, Keiko; Christine's husband, Andrea, and sons, Adriano and Marcello; and Heidi's husband, Mark Helfand, whose love and encouragement make all our work possible and worthwhile.

Chapter 1

Getting Started

In this chapter, we discuss the features of the Internet and introduce the main reasons we think the Internet should be used in English teaching.

Language. Writing. Print. These are the three great revolutionary developments in communication and cognition, each one ushering in a new level of human civilization. And now we are in the midst of another revolution in human communication, based on the development and spread of computers and the Internet.

Just as the development of the printing press 500 years ago dramatically expanded the information available to individuals and society, the development of the Internet is doing so today. With a single computer and a telephone line, a young child in a rural village can access more information today than was available by any means to the greatest scientists of the world a century ago.

The Internet is reshaping nearly all aspects of society. On-line advertising, marketing, and sales are growing at exponential rates and shaking up the world's financial markets. Many schools in the developed countries are now wired for the Internet, inspiring grassroots efforts to reform education in order to take better advantage of information technology. A majority of university students and professors in the industrialized countries use the Internet to share ideas, conduct research, and collaborate in the production of knowledge. Music, media, politics, entertainment—name the field, and it is being transformed by the Internet.

Nor are all these changes taking place only in the wealthier countries. Many developing countries rightly view the Internet as a potential tool for leapfrogging to higher stages of information access and economic development. Individuals, institutions, and governments in emerging economies are putting substantial resources into computers and the Internet, and the fastest growing computer markets in the world are in places like China and Egypt. It is only a matter of time before students in much of the world will have at least some access to the Internet and will need to use it for a wide range of personal and occupational reasons once they graduate (see Figure 1).

Features of the Internet

The Internet encompasses many different ways of communicating and exchanging information. For the most part, though, they can be categorized as *asynchronous computer-mediated communication, synchronous computer-mediated communication,* and *hypertext* (see Table 1).

ASYNCHRONOUS COMPUTER-MEDIATED COMMUNICATION

Computer-mediated communication (CMC) refers to communication that takes place via networked computers. Asynchronous CMC refers to CMC that takes place in a delayed fashion; in other words, the people communicating do not need to be sitting at the computer at the same time. Rather, messages are somehow deposited to be read later.

Figure 1. Worldwide Internet Growth

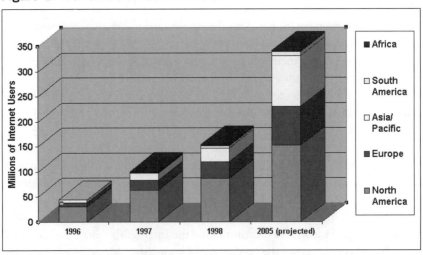

Sources: *Computer Economics Projects Worldwide Internet Users* (1999); "How Many Online?" (n.d.).

TABLE 1. Main Internet Features

Feature	Examples	What You Can Do
Asynchronous computer-mediated communication	E-mail Web bulletin boards	Write a message for others to read later
Synchronous computer-mediated communication	Chat rooms Instant messaging Videoconferencing	Communicate in real time with others who are on-line at the same time
Hypertext	World Wide Web	Access and publish multimedia documents with clickable links to other documents

The most common form of asynchronous CMC is electronic mail, now referred to almost exclusively as *e-mail*. E-mail is usually used to send simple text messages but can also be used to exchange formatted documents (including word-processed documents, sound files, pictures, computer software, and even full-motion video) as attachments. E-mail can be exchanged one-to-one, or many-to-many through e-mail discussion lists. On these lists, which can include anywhere from a handful of participants to tens of thousands, any participant can send a message that will be automatically forwarded to all others, thus facilitating group discussion. To become a member of an e-mail discussion group, you have to send a subscription message per the requirements of that particular list.

Another popular form of asynchronous CMC is bulletin boards accessed through the World Wide Web. To post or read a message on a Web bulletin board, no subscription is required (though some World Wide Web sites may ask you to fill out a registration form first). In most cases, anyone coming to the Web site can read through or post messages. In addition, these messages are listed in *threaded* form (i.e., organized by topic) on the site rather than sent in chronological order to individuals, as in e-mail discussion lists.

Asynchronous CMC, in particular e-mail, remains the mother of all Internet applications. No matter what else you can do on the Internet, communicating with friends and colleagues remains the most popular Net-based activity, and nothing beats the convenience of doing so via e-mail. As will be seen throughout this book, e-mail and other forms of asynchronous CMC are a powerful way of connecting students and educators.

SYNCHRONOUS COMPUTER-MEDIATED COMMUNICATION

In *synchronous* (or *real-time*) CMC, all participants must be sitting at the computer at the same time. Messages are sent instantly, and communication takes place live, as on a telephone. As with asynchronous CMC, communication can be either one-to-one or many-to-many.

Several types of synchronous CMC will be discussed in this book. The most common type is Internet-based *chat,* which takes place in chat rooms found on the Internet (e.g., *Talk City,* http://www.talkcity.com, or the discussion forums found at *Dave's ESL Cafe,* http://eslcafe.com) or on a one-to-one or small-group basis using software such as ICQ (read "I seek you") (1999; see http://www.icq.com) or AOL Instant Messenger (1999; see http://www.aol.com/aim). A closely related medium for real-time group discussion is called a *MOO,* where participants can not only communicate but also engage in simulated activity, such as moving from room to room or examining objects.

In addition to these free, Internet-based chat programs, a particular type of commercial software enables real-time communication in a single setting. One of the best known of these products is Daedalus InterChange (a component of Daedalus Integrated Writing Environment, 1997; see http://www.daedalus.com), which allows people in a computer laboratory to discuss ideas using a convenient split-screen interface.

Real-time on-line communication can take place not only with text but also with voice or video. Conferencing software such as Microsoft NetMeeting (1999; see http://www.microsoft.com/netmeeting) or CU-SeeMe (1998; see http://www.wpine.com/Products/CU-SeeMe) allows students to communicate in real time using audio, video, text, or white boards.

HYPERTEXT

The Internet is more than a communication medium—it is also a worldwide repository of linked multimedia documents, brought together on the World Wide Web. There are now tens of millions of pages on the Web, bringing together reports, advertisements, personal home pages, and every other kind of information known to humankind.

The World Wide Web is based on principles of *hypertext,* a nonlinear, linked or layered form of information organization whereby documents in a database are connected via *hyperlinks.* On the Web, pointing and clicking the mouse on a link brings you to a connected document elsewhere. The World Wide Web includes not only textual information and links but also documents based on graphics, audio, and video. Technically, these documents are referred to as *hypermedia,* but the words *hypertext* and *hypermedia* are used interchangeably.

The World Wide Web allows unprecedented access to information by computer users throughout the world. It also allows inexpensive international publishing; any classroom with access to the Internet can now publish for free its own newsletter, report, or magazine using advertising-supported Web-publishing sites such as *XOOM.com* (http://xoom.com) or *Yahoo! GeoCities* (http://www.geocities.yahoo.com).

The various formats of the Internet are merging and evolving. With new graphical software, e-mail messages themselves can include hyperlinks to other information, thus becoming a form of hypertext. The World Wide Web includes not only hypertext documents but also software for sending and receiving e-mail (e.g., *Hotmail,* http://www.hotmail.com; *Yahoo! Mail,* http://mail.yahoo.com). Many sites on the Web, such as *Dave's ESL Cafe* (http://eslcafe.com), include forums for synchronous and asynchronous communication. Which of the many Internet features you use will depend on your goals, but once you start using the Internet, you will probably begin to take advantage of all the features it has to offer.

The First Steps

What, then, do you need to start using the Internet for English teaching? The basic necessities are (a) access to a computer, (b) a means of connecting to the Internet, (c) an Internet account, and (d) an e-mail address.

ACCESS TO A COMPUTER

Virtually any personal computer, no matter how new or old, can be used to connect to the Internet. Models of computers dating from before 1996 may have difficulty with some of the graphical or multimedia features of the Internet, but even these computers can be used for text-based communication, such as via e-mail. If your main interest is in using the Internet, there is no need to purchase a high-end computer.

Today, an increasing number of other devices can also be used to access the Internet. Microsoft WebTV (see http://www.webtv.com) provides one inexpensive way to access the Internet, and even some telephones can connect. But with personal computers costing less than ever before and many schools, colleges, and public libraries providing some computer access, you'll probably want to take advantage of the many features for creating, saving, and printing files that are best done with a computer.

MEANS OF CONNECTING TO THE INTERNET

Most colleges and universities in industrialized countries, and increasingly in developing countries, maintain a permanent connection to the Internet via cabling or satellite. There are several options for connecting to the Internet from home. The most common is via a telephone line and a small piece of equipment called a *modem.* Modems come as standard equipment with many personal computers today; otherwise they can be purchased inexpensively. The faster the baud rate of the modem, the faster it allows you to send or receive data from the Internet. Having a fast modem can be a big convenience, especially in countries where local telephone calls are billed by the minute.

In some countries, other options are available for connecting to the Internet. These include special leased telephone lines, integrated services digital network

(ISDN) telephone lines, cable modems (via television cable networks), and satellite connections. Ask colleagues or local Internet service providers (ISPs) what kinds of connections are available in your area. Keep in mind that even though services such as cable modems may have a higher start-up cost or monthly fee, they may save you money on telephone bills and give you the convenience of a 24-hour-per-day connection.

AN INTERNET ACCOUNT

If you want to connect to the Internet from home via a modem and telephone line, you'll need an Internet account. An Internet account will provide you with a *userid* (user identification, pronounced "user eye dee") and password so you can dial up and connect to the Internet through your modem. Basic Internet accounts are free in some countries if you are willing to see advertisements displayed on your screen; otherwise, they usually cost U.S.$15–40 per month in various parts of the world. To connect to the Internet, your modem will dial a local telephone number (unless you have a nontelephone system, such as one that uses cable modems or satellites), so keep in mind that the local telephone costs will add to your bill.

People working at universities, at colleges, and in many public school systems are provided with Internet accounts for free. These accounts will allow you to access the Internet from computers at your school or office. In some cases, you will also be given free dial-up access, so you can call in from home to use the Internet without a monthly fee.

AN E-MAIL ADDRESS

Although you can use the Internet in some ways (e.g., finding information on the World Wide Web) without an e-mail address, e-mail is such a useful and valuable tool that you will surely want one or more addresses. If you get an Internet account from an ISP, you will be provided with an e-mail address. Likewise, many universities and school districts that provide Internet access will give you an e-mail address.

If you have access to the Internet but don't have an e-mail account, you can use one of the many free e-mail services on the World Wide Web, with the two best being *Yahoo! Mail* (http://mail.yahoo.com) and *Hotmail* (http://www .hotmail.com). These services are also useful for setting up a second account to use when you are away from your home or office but might have access to the Internet. If your regular e-mail account offers downloading from other locations (i.e., if it is a point-of-presence, or POP, account), you can even use *Yahoo! Mail* or *Hotmail* to read the e-mail from your regular account.

The Internet and English Teaching

In our view, there are five main reasons to use the Internet for English teaching. Taken together, these reasons help bring English teaching ALIVE (see Figure 2):

1. *authenticity:* Language learning is most successful when it takes place in authentic, meaningful contexts. The Internet is a low-cost method of making language learning meaningful; it gives students 24-hour access to vast amounts of authentic material on any topic they are interested in and allows opportunities for authentic communication and publishing.

2. *literacy:* The ability to read, write, communicate, research, and publish on the Internet represents important new forms of literacy needed in the 21st century. By combining English and technology in the classroom, you will help your students master the skills they will need for academic and occupational success.

3. *interaction:* Interaction is the major means of acquiring a language and gaining fluency. All effective English teaching incorporates some kind of interactive communication in the curriculum. The Internet provides opportunities for students to interact 24 hours a day with native and nonnative speakers from around the world.

4. *vitality:* Too often, classrooms are reflective of *T.E.N.O.R.* (teaching English for no obvious reason; see Medgyes, 1986), as students get bogged down in memorizing grammar rules or decontextualized vocabulary. The Internet can inject an element of vitality into teaching and motivate students as they communicate in a medium that is flexible, multimodal, constantly changing, and connected to their real-life needs.

5. *empowerment:* Mastery of the Internet increases the personal power of teachers and students. It allows them to become autonomous lifelong

Figure 2. Help Your Classroom Come Alive

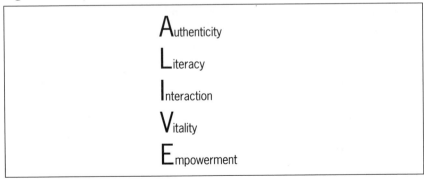

learners who can find what they need when they need it and collaborate with others to help construct new knowledge. By mastering the Internet, teachers and students can become shapers of the multimedia future.

One caveat: Though the Internet provides a valuable medium for helping bring classrooms alive, successful results depend on how the Internet is used. Just as students won't learn simply by being brought to a classroom, neither will they learn by being sat down in front of a networked computer. In the end, it is not the technology itself but the teaching that makes the difference. In fact, because of the complexity of the medium, using the Internet well is especially important. So don't look to the Internet as a quick fix for all the problems that your students face. Do be prepared for a lot of hard work and frustration that come from trying to use a new and evolving medium. But also be prepared for the rewards of helping your students master new technologies to communicate with peers around the world.

About This Book

After reading this chapter, you will be ready to get started. In the chapters that follow, you will find information that we hope will enrich your teaching and your students' learning experiences.

Chapter 2 focuses on the Internet resources most valuable to teachers of English. We direct you to a wealth of sites and information to assist your professional development, collegial networking, and day-to-day classroom needs.

In the following three chapters, we focus on three major skill areas that are being reshaped by the Internet: communication and collaboration, reading and research, and writing and publishing. Chapter 3 introduces ways of using the Internet to improve your students' communicative ability and involve them in collaborative interaction with learners around the world. Chapter 4 introduces the new research skills that are needed in the age of the Internet and helps you find appropriate ways to teach them. Chapter 5 examines how writing and authorship are changing in the on-line era and discusses ways of organizing student publishing projects in the English language classroom.

Chapter 6 addresses the topic of distance education, focusing on distance-learning opportunities for learners and teachers of English. The chapter also discusses some of the controversies that have arisen over who controls distance education and how that affects educational quality. In chapter 7, we examine how all the elements discussed in this book can be combined in a coherent curricular package, and we profile four teachers who have had success in integrating the Internet into their teaching. In chapter 8, we discuss approaches to researching language learning in on-line environments and survey the research that has been conducted to date.

Supplement: How to Make Web Pages is a complete guide to the basics of creating and storing pages on the World Wide Web. It is followed by a list of references cited. Appendix A is an alphabetical index of the Internet addresses for all the Web sites mentioned in the book. Appendixes B and C list the most important books and journals, respectively, for further reading on the topic of the Internet in English language teaching. Finally, a glossary (Appendix D) defines important terms related to the Internet.

Throughout the book, we provide you with many suggestions and ideas for using the Internet in English teaching. We also point you to hundreds of Internet resources from which you can get further information. Other than a personal computer and an Internet connection, and your own creativity and perseverance, we hope in this book to provide everything else you need to make your classroom come alive.

Resources for Teachers

In this chapter, we discuss how English language teachers can use the Internet to communicate with colleagues and find professional resources.

Professional development is the lifeblood of teaching. Educators are constantly experimenting with new methods, approaches, techniques, and materials. They attend regional and international conferences, participate in in-service workshops, read and submit articles to professional magazines and journals, and seek other ways to exchange ideas with and learn from colleagues. However, these activities often take a great deal of time, energy, and money.

The Internet now provides another medium—often faster, easier, and less expensive than other ways—to draw on many of the same resources. Access to the Internet increases the materials and resources available to educators as well as the opportunities for professional networking and exchange of ideas. Indeed, perhaps the most valuable contribution of the Internet to English language teaching is its role in facilitating teachers' access to professional material, contacts, and resources.

In the first section of this chapter, we focus on the uses of e-mail communication. We then discuss the role of resources on the World Wide Web. We hope the suggestions presented in this chapter will inspire practicing teachers to explore new venues for communication, dialogue, and development.

E-Mail: Creating a Global Network

E-mail allows teachers to communicate rapidly and inexpensively with colleagues throughout the world, developing an invaluable global network. The expanding availability of e-mail and other technologies has made communication among colleagues much easier, whether they are in the same institution or on different sides of the world.

You can make connections with other teachers by sending them an e-mail of introduction. E-mail addresses can be found attached to many journal articles, Web sites, and other publications, such as the program books for professional conferences. (See Figure 1 for a sample message to the author of an article.) The program book for TESOL's annual convention, for example, includes the e-mail addresses of all presenters. This information is especially valuable if you are unable to attend a particular session and wish to get in touch with the presenter.

COLLABORATION AMONG TEACHERS

Sometimes collaborative conference presentations, journal articles, and even books are planned and written entirely on-line. This book is a prime example. It was discussed and written almost entirely through the exchange of e-mail messages. A lot of questions, answers, ideas, and challenges were shared throughout the writing process, and many word-processed documents (usually drafts of chapters) were exchanged as e-mail attachments. Indeed, as we wrote this book, we were constantly reminded that collaborative projects involve long-distance dialogue, cooperation, and decision making.

Another example of teacher collaboration via e-mail takes place through interclass projects. These projects are usually planned via e-mail, especially if the teachers involved are in locations that are distant from each other. The interclass projects described in chapters 3 and 5 illustrate the use of e-mail correspondence during the planning, implementation, and evaluation phases. In the message shown in Figure 2, a teacher in China shares her excitement about and her hopes for the Cities Project (see Hess, 1995, http://www.nyu.edu/pages/hess/cities.html) with one of the other teachers involved.

E-mail communication can be exciting but also challenging. Miscommunication can arise when discussants lack the emotional clues that are normally expressed through intonation or facial expressions. And teachers can be overwhelmed by the task of managing a large number of e-mail messages. The tips given in Figure 3 are designed to help you use e-mail effectively.

COMMUNICATION AND NETWORKING VIA E-MAIL LISTS

The power of e-mail is magnified manifold through e-mail lists. Also called *e-mail discussion lists, listservers,* or *listservs* (after the proprietary Listserv software

Figure 1. Message to an Author

What do you do if you find a reference but can't find the full-text article? Most authors receive offprints of their articles from the publisher, and many are willing to send them out in response to informed and polite requests. See the sample message below.

```
To:       Mark Warschauer (markw@hawaii.edu)
From:     Hua Shao Wen
          (huasw@mailbox.shanghai.edu.cn)
Date:     February 12, 1999
Subject:  Online Learning in Sociocultural Context

Dear Dr. Warschauer:

I am a graduate student in TEFL at Shanghai
University. I am planning to do my master's research
on online language learning. I have read your book,
E-Mail for English Teaching, and found it very
helpful for my studies.

I came across a reference to one of your papers,
Online Learning in Sociocultural Context, which was
published in 1998 in Anthropology & Education
Quarterly. I think this article would be very helpful
to my research, but unfortunately the journal is not
available in China. Is it by any chance possible that
you could send me a copy of the paper, either
electronically (as e-mail text or as an e-mail
attachment) or in hard copy? My contact information
is listed below.

Thank you very much for your kind attention. If you
would like to see a paper I wrote about Internet use
in Chinese universities, I will be happy to send it
to you.

Shao Wen

Hua Shao Wen
Department of Foreign Languages
Shanghai University
Shanghai, China
e-mail: huasw@mailbox.shanghai.edu.cn
```

Figure 2. Message to a Colleague About the Cities Project (Hess, 1995)

```
DATE SENT: Friday, February 27, 1998 7:59 AM
FROM:     Peiya Gu
          pygu@nsad.suda.edu/cn
TO:       Christine Meloni
          <meloni@gwis2.circ.gwu.edu>
SUBJECT:  RE: The Cities Project Begins!

Hi, Christine,

You're working fast! My students just finished their
first introduction and are waiting impatiently for the
responses. So far only two follow-ups.

While my students are learning about Washington, I
guess your students could learn about Suzhou, a very
beautiful ancient 'Garden City' in China. Maybe
someday you want to come for a visit too :-)

I wish all of our students would get involved in this
natural learning process and really produce sth to
their satisfaction. I've two TAs who're helping with
the project and maybe sometimes they'll write you
about the interactions between our sts.

See you,
Peiya
```

that runs many of them), e-mail lists allow dozens, hundreds, or even thousands of people throughout the world to communicate with each other.

Some e-mail lists serve as newsletters, allowing one-way communication from the owner of the list to the recipients. For example, *O-Hayo Sensei* (http:// www.ohayosensei.com) announces teaching jobs in Japan. *Daily Brief* (http:// www.incinc.net) contains highly digested news delivered daily to the subscriber's in-box. *Papyrus News* (Warschauer, n.d., http://www.lll.hawaii.edu/web/faculty /markw/papyrus-news.html) includes articles and messages about the global impact of information technology on language, literacy, and education. *Edupage* (n.d., http://www.educause.edu/pub/edupage/edupage.html) is another newsletter about education and technology, with short summaries of recent newspaper and magazine articles. *Red Rock Eater News Service* (Agre, n.d., http://dlis

Figure 3. Top 10 Tips for Using E-Mail Effectively

1. *clarity:* Keep your message simple and clear. Start off with a short, easy-to-understand subject line. Then express one or two ideas at the most, in short paragraphs, with blank lines between paragraphs. If you have more than two points to address, write a second message.

2. *replies:* Don't use the "reply to all" function if only one person needs to read the response. And when you reply to a message, don't automatically quote all the material from the received e-mail message. Rather, either summarize that message's key point or quote only the points that need to be mentioned.

3. *cc: and bcc:* Use the *cc:* (carbon copy) function to send a public copy to someone. Use *bcc:* (blind cc) to send a private copy to someone. If you need to send messages to a big group of people, put their addresses on the *bcc:* line instead of the *cc:* line. That way, they'll receive a smaller header, and no one can accidentally reply to all the other recipients.

4. *flaming:* The rapid exchange of e-mail, together with its relative anonymity, often leads to hostile language known as *flaming.* The best way to respond to flaming is to ignore it. If you feel like firing off a hostile message yourself, go ahead and write it—but leave it in your out-box overnight. Then delete it the next day without even reading it.

5. *spam:* Your colleagues will not appreciate receiving chain letters, unconfirmed virus hoaxes (see Figure 7 in this chapter), and copies of commercial advertisements. Resist the temptation to send them on, especially in messages to groups.

6. *attachments:* Send attachments only when the information cannot reasonably be included as part of the message. Never send an attachment to an e-mail discussion list.

7. *filters:* Most e-mail software is set up so that it can automatically filter your incoming messages into separate folders. For example, you can have all your mail for *TESL-L* or all the mail from your assistant dean automatically filed into a special folder when it arrives. Take the time and effort to set your filters up for convenient organization of your messages. This is especially important for managing the large number of messages that you get when you subscribe to e-mail lists.

8. *signatures:* Most e-mail software allows you to attach an optional signature file, including such items as your name, address, e-mail address, Web address, and institution, to the bottom of messages. Some software also allows you to alternate several signatures. Use signatures if you wish, but keep them short and simple.

9. *privacy:* Your e-mail messages might be read by your computer systems operator, your boss, or someone standing over the recipient's shoulder. Or the recipient may intentionally or accidentally forward your message to another

person or even to a list of thousands. Don't write anything in e-mail that would embarrass you if it were published in the newspaper.

10. *netiquette:* Be kind and easygoing on-line. Avoid long-winded "I win/you lose" discussions. Compliment your colleagues and cc their bosses. Use a bit of humor. Soften your opinions by adding *that's my two cents* or *IMHO* (in my humble opinion). Add a smiley :-) to your message.

For more tips on using e-mail, see the *Netiquette Home Page* (Rinaldi, 1998, http://www.fau.edu/netiquette/netiquette.html) and *Resources for Moderators and Facilitators of Online Discussions* (Collins & Berge, 2000, http://www.emoderators .com/moderators.shtml).

.gseis.ucla.edu/people/pagre/rre.html) provides information on the sociology of the Internet, including articles and information on the relationship of computing to politics, economics, education, and culture.

The other type of e-mail list is usually referred to as an *e-mail discussion list.* With this type of electronic list, two-way communication takes place. The people subscribed to the e-mail list not only receive messages but can also send them to all the recipients of the list. Most lists also offer an archive service so that subscribers can retrieve past postings from a central location.

Hundreds of electronic lists are available in a wide variety of subject areas, including English language teaching, linguistics, literature, foreign languages, educational computer technology, and virtually any content area (e.g. the environment, health care, public transportation). By joining and participating in e-mail lists, educators can carry out a dialogue on subjects of interest to them with people in all parts of the world.

E-mail discussion lists are usually organized in one of two ways: *moderated* or *unmoderated.* The list managers determine the rules and regulations for the list. They decide whether they want all the messages to pass through them before they are posted (moderated), or whether they want to give each subscriber the ability to post messages directly to the list without prior approval of the content (unmoderated). Each format has its advantages and disadvantages. Lists that are moderated take more time to manage, but they save the subscribers the bother of receiving messages that might be considered *spam* (messages that are off-topic, flames, or commercial plugs). These messages are annoyances on lists and at times can stifle the discussion that is taking place. Managers of lists that are *unmoderated* don't screen the messages individually, which gives more conversational power to each subscriber but can allow for the passage of inappropriate messages that might insult or irritate others.

E-mail discussion lists run under a variety of software, with some of the most common being Listserv, Listproc, and Majordomo. This software resides on the host computer and is not needed by the end user. However, depending on the particular software, the list may require you to use different expressions for commands. In any case, when you subscribe to a list, you will immediately be sent an e-mail message that explains to you the most important commands for further communication (e.g., how to subscribe and unsubscribe) for that particular system. It is important to read over the welcome message carefully and save it for future reference.

In the sections that follow, we describe some e-mail lists that are of potential interest to English language teachers

TESL-L

TESL-L (see Kitao & Kitao, 1999b, http://www.ling.lancs.ac.uk/staff/visitors /kenji/lis-tesl.htm), a moderated list with more than 20,000 subscribers, is one of the largest professional e-mail lists in the world. *TESL-L* was established in 1991 and brings together English teachers from more than 120 countries. Subscribers may send messages on any topic relating to the teaching of English to the list if the messages adhere to the rules given to subscribers. *TESL-L* subscribers who want to participate in discussions on more specialized topics may choose to join one of the sublists:

- *TESLCA-L:* technology, computers, and English language teaching
- *TESLFF-L:* fluency first and whole language approaches
- *TESLIE-L:* intensive English programs, teaching, and administration
- *TESLJB-L:* jobs, employment, and working conditions in English language teaching
- *TESLMW-L:* material writers
- *TESP-L:* English for specific purposes

To subscribe to *TESL-L* or one of its branch lists, send an e-mail message to listserv@cunyvm.cuny.edu. Leave the subject line blank; in the body of the message, write "subscribe TESL-L Yourfirstname Yourlastname" (without the quotation marks). For example, here is the e-mail message that Heidi Shetzer would send to subscribe to *TESL-L:*

```
To:         listserv@cunyvm.cuny.edu
From:       "Heidi Shetzer" <hshetzer@ix.netcom.com>
Subject:
Date:       Fri, 10 March 1999 11:41:35

subscribe TESL-L Heidi Shetzer
```

Once subscribed to *TESL-L,* you will discover that many discussions are taking place (see Figure 4 for a typical message). The new subscriber might consider first *lurking* (i.e., listening quietly) before sending a message to the list.

Figure 4. A Typical Message on *TESL-L*

```
Date:       Wed, 21 Jul 1999 04:43:03 B1000
From:       AL-KALBANI
            <N.S.H.Al-Kalbani@NEWCASTLE. AC.UK>
Subject:    speaking and writing abilities, are they
            related?
To:         TESL-L@CUNYVM.CUNY.EDU

Hi TESL-Lers,

I was wondering if any of you has come across any
studies which have looked into the correlation between
speaking and writing abilities. In other words, to
what extent can one make predictions about a
student's ability in writing based on that student's
level in speaking and vice versa?
Thanks in advance.

Miss Najat AL-Kalbani
Language Centre
University of Newcastle Upon Tyne
UK
n.s.h.al-kalbani@ncl.ac.uk
```

TESL-L has a large archive, organized by topic, that subscribers can access and use to enhance their learning and teaching. List members can send commands to the server to learn about the contents of the archive, and to access and have copies of files from the archive delivered to their e-mail in-boxes. Files in the archive include, for example, information about upcoming conferences, papers that have been written and contributed by list members, and archived discussions on a variety of topics that range from teaching grammar to teaching with music. The list's welcome message contains further information about this feature.

TESL-L is an extremely active list, with subscribers posting a large number of messages each day. To make reading easier, you may want to set your *TESL-L* options to *digest* by sending the message "set TESL-L digest" to listserv @cunyvm.cuny.edu after you subscribe. In digest mode, each day's messages will be grouped and sent to you in one large e-mail message per day.

You will also want to stop receiving mail temporarily when you are on vacation or away from your e-mail. You can do that by sending the message "set TESL-L nomail" to listserv@cunyvm.cuny.edu.

To subscribe to any of the *TESL-L* branches listed above, you must first become a member of *TESL-L*. However, once you have subscribed to the sublist, you can set the main *TESL-L* list to *nomail* if you do not want to receive messages from the main list.

Finally, you must send messages to one address when communicating with the *TESL-L* computer (listserv@cunyvm.cuny.edu; e.g., to set options such as *digest* or *nomail*) and another when communicating with the *TESL-L* membership (TESL-L@cunyvm.cuny.edu; e.g., to post a message). This distinction is important for *TESL-L* and for all other e-mail discussion lists.

Other Lists for English Language Teachers

Because the majority of *TESL-L* subscribers are in higher education, *TESLK-12* was established especially for K–12 teachers. It is a sister list of *TESL-L* but not a formal branch of it. To become a member of *TESLK-12*, send the e-mail message "subscribe TESLK-12 Yourfirstname Yourlastname" to listserv@cunyvm .cuny.edu.

NETEACH-L (see Moody, n.d., http://www.ilc.cuhk.edu.hk/english/neteach /main.html) is a very active, friendly list focusing on the use of the Internet in English teaching. As you read this book and afterward, *NETEACH-L* will be a valuable resource for establishing and maintaining contact with other teachers interested in the same topic. To subscribe to this list, send an e-mail message to listproc@ukans.edu with "subscribe NETEACH-L Yourfirstname Yourlastname" written in the body.

In addition to the discussion on *NETEACH-L,* subscribers have access to extensive archives and to *Sites Neteachers Thought Were Cool!* (Pfaff-Harris, 1999, http://www.linguistic-funland.com/neteach.html). "Neteachers" also meet regularly for real-time Internet chats, as announced on the list. Using *NETEACH-L,* subscribers can ask questions and expect speedy and useful responses. Questions might include nontechnical ones, such as "Where can I find tongue twisters on the Web?" "What about intercultural awareness activities for the classroom?" or "Does anyone have experience with electronic portfolios?" In addition, users might ask more technical questions, such as "How can I put audio files on my Web pages?" or "What are your experiences with distance education and language teaching?"

Other lists of potential interest to educators in the field of English language teaching include *TEFL China, ELT-ASIA, CONTENT-ESL,* and *LLTI-L. TEFL China* is a list for the discussion of living and teaching English in China, Taiwan, Hong Kong, and Macao. On the list's Web site, *TEFL China Tea House* (http:// teflchina.com), people can post their experiences and suggestions. To subscribe, send a blank message (i.e., with nothing written in the body) to teflchina-subscribe@topica.com.

ELTASIA-L (Tantsetthi, Williams, & Reynolds, n.d., http://www.nectec.or.th

/users/ttesol/eltasia.htm) is a list for teachers of English in all parts of Asia. According to the list's welcome message, "The purpose of ELTASIA-L is to provide an international scholarly forum and central archive to facilitate and coordinate the discussion, research, documentation, and dissemination of information on the teaching and learning of English in Asia." To subscribe, send an e-mail message to majordomo@nectec.or.th with "subscribe ELT-ASIA" in the body.

CONTENT-ESL (Kasper, 1999, http://members.aol.com/Drlfk/Content-ESL.html) exists to (a) provide a forum for the discussion of teaching English with content, (b) provide opportunities for finding partners for content-related projects, and (c) share ideas and resources for content-based language teaching. The list also holds monthly chat sessions for members. To subscribe to this list, send a blank message to content-esl-subscribe@egroups.com.

LLTI-L, the *Language Learning Technology International List* (Foelsche, 1995, http://iall.net/LLTI.html), is for people interested in managing language learning laboratories or discussing their setup or reconfiguration. A glance through the archives on the list's Web site shows a variety of technical questions related to software and hardware. To subscribe, send a message to listserv @dartmouth.edu with the message "subscribe llti Yourfirstname Yourlastname" in the body.

Linguistics Lists

LINGUIST, a moderated list begun in 1994 and sponsored by Eastern Michigan University and Wayne State University, is an outstanding resource for people interested in linguistics. An interesting feature of this list is the degree to which subscribers summarize postings. For instance, a list member will post a query to the list and, after receiving responses directly, will most likely post a summary of those responses to the list. This practice enriches all the list subscribers: The responses otherwise would not reach all subscribers, as they were sent directly to the individual as opposed to everyone on the list. *LINGUIST*'s companion Web site (http://www.linguistlist.org) contains links to a multitude of resources related to theoretical and applied linguistics, an extensive archive of messages posted to the list, and instructions for subscribing to the list.

Other lists of interest to linguists are *LTEST-L, SLART-L,* and *LANG-USE.* LTEST-L (n.d., http://www.surrey.ac.uk/ELI/ltest-l.html), which is associated with the International Language Testing Association (http://www.surrey.ac.uk /ELI/ilta/ilta.html), is a list related to the topic of language testing theory, research, and practice. To subscribe, send an e-mail message to listserv@psuvm .psu.edu with "subscribe ltest-l Yourfirstname Yourlastname" in the body.

SLART-L (*Second Language Acquisition Research and Teaching List,* n.d., http://listserv.cuny.edu/archives/slart-l.html) brings together people interested in applied linguistics. To subscribe, send an e-mail message to listserv@cunyvm .cuny.edu. with "subscribe slart-l Yourfirstname Yourlastname" in the body.

LANG-USE also addresses issues related to research on language acquisition and use. To subscribe to the list, send an e-mail message to listserv@vm.temple.edu with "subscribe lang-use Yourfirstname Yourlastname" in the body.

Foreign Language Lists

English language teachers have a great deal in common with teachers of other languages, so electronic lists for language teachers can be useful to them. *FLTEACH* (see LeLoup & Ponterio, 1995, http://www.cortland.edu/flteach) is one list for people interested in the teaching of foreign languages in general. Teachers of languages from Spanish to Swahili can exchange teaching ideas and strategies with others on this high-volume list, partially supported by the National Endowment for the Humanities. To subscribe to *FLTEACH,* send an e-mail message to listserv@listserv.acsu.buffalo.edu with "subscribe flteach Yourfirstname Yourlastname" in the body.

Managing and Finding Other Lists

Electronic lists abound. By some counts the number might be close to 100,000. How do you find a list on a particular subject? Probably the best known directories of electronic lists are *Liszt* (http://www.liszt.com) and *Tile.Net* (http:// tile.net). At *Liszt,* for instance, you can search the main directory or limit your search to 1 of 17 topic areas (e.g., books, education, music, science). Another resource for finding out about lists is *NEW-LIST* (1999, http://scout.cs.wisc.edu /scout/caservices/new-list), a list of new lists that features a searchable archive on its Web site.

Be judicious in signing up for electronic lists. Immediately joining every list that promises to be of professional or personal interest could be disastrous. Remember that every message written by a subscriber to the list will end up in your mailbox. We recommend that you first subscribe to only one or two lists, try them out, and then decide whether to stay subscribed or to unsubscribe depending on the volume of e-mail messages you are able to manage.

Finally, and most important, please note that you can form your own list to arrange communication among colleagues or even your students. Many univer- sities or school districts have software for starting lists; ask the personnel in your institution's computer department. In any case, there are a number of sites on the Web where you can start and manage your own list free of charge if you are willing to accept short advertisements attached to the bottom of the e-mail messages. One of the best of these services is *eGroups.com* (http://www .egroups.com).

World Wide Web: Discovering a Gold Mine of Resources

The World Wide Web contains millions of documents from organizations and individuals all over the world. You as a teacher can find a wealth of resources on the World Wide Web, including full-text journal articles, conference presentations, book reviews, lesson plans, actual handouts for classroom use, lists of print and electronic journals, home pages of English language teachers, lists of associations, and much more. But just as is true when panning for gold, trying to find exactly what you are looking for on the Web can be frustrating, challenging, and time-consuming. To get you started, we list a large number of resources of interest to teachers below. (See chapter 4 for a discussion of strategies for searching the Web.)

PROFESSIONAL JOURNALS AND MAGAZINES

Some professional journals are now published entirely on-line. On-line journals of interest to English language professionals include *TESL-EJ* (http://www.kyoto-su.ac.jp/information/tesl-ej), which focuses on the theory and practice of language teaching; *The Internet TESL Journal* (http://www.aitech.ac.jp/~iteslj), which includes short, practical articles; *Language Learning & Technology* (http://polyglot.cal.msu.edu/llt), a research journal for second language educators; *CALL-EJ Online* (http://www.lerc.ritsumei.ac.jp/callej), which covers computer-assisted language learning (CALL); and *Kairos* (http://english.ttu.edu/kairos), a journal on computers and writing.

Other professional journals and magazines publish part of their contents on-line. *ESL Magazine* (http://www.eslmag.com) posts the column "Christine Meloni's NetWorthy" on the Web as well as occasional feature articles, such as "The Internet in the Classroom" (Meloni, 1998a, http://www.eslmag.com /Article.html). *American Language Review* (http://www.alr.org) publishes its back issues on-line, as does *English Teaching Forum* (http://e.usia.gov/forum).

Many journals that do not publish on-line make their tables of contents or abstracts of articles available on a Web site. Journals that provide on-line abstracts include *The Modern Language Journal* (http://polyglot.lss.wisc.edu/mlj), *The Language Teacher* (http://langue.hyper.chubu.ac.jp/jalt/pub/tlt), *ELT Journal* (http://www3.oup.co.uk/eltj), *International Review of Applied Linguistics in Language Teaching* (http://www3.oup.co.uk/iral), and *TESOL Quarterly* (http:// www.tesol.org).

VIRTUAL LIBRARIES

Virtual libraries include the full text of articles from magazines and newspapers and other information that is found in libraries; users are usually charged a fee. For example, *UnCoverWeb* (http://uncweb.carl.org) is a commercial service allowing users to find and order full-text articles from more than 18,000 academic journals in a wide variety of disciplines. Articles are faxed to any telephone number in the world for a fee. The main Web site of the Educational Resource Information Center (ERIC, http://www.accesseric.org) includes searchable databases, as does *AskERIC* (n.d., http://ericir.syr.edu). Users can search for abstracts of thousands of articles on education research published since 1966 and order documents on a pay-per-article basis.

For a monthly subscription charge, *Electric Library* (http://www.elibrary.com) provides its users with on-line access to the full text of articles from newspapers, magazines, journals, and news wires; transcripts; maps; pictures; and other documents. Check with your institution or local library to see if it has a subscription to this resource, or open an individual account if you desire. *NewsLibrary* (http://www.newslibrary.com), another on-line library, lets visitors search on-line newspapers from across the United States, charging a fee for each article viewed in full text. *Northern Light* (http://northernlight.com) also has full-text articles available through the "pay-per-view" method.

Berkeley Digital Library SunSITE (http://sunsite.berkeley.edu) provides information on library databases throughout the world, including a useful page called *Libweb* (2000, http://sunsite.berkeley.edu/Libweb), which lists Web-accessible library servers located in more than 70 countries. *LIBCAT* (Noonan, 1999, http://www.metronet.lib.mn.us/lc/lc1.cfm) is another excellent resource to consult about various library Web sites, public databases, and special collections that are accessible from the Internet.

ON-LINE MEDIA

An abundance of English language media resources are available on the Web. *Project Gutenberg* (http://www.gutenberg.net) is a sizable collection of free literary materials, including works of nonfiction, novels, poetry, and plays. Additional reading resources are found in *Digital Libraries Initiative* (http://www.dli2.nsf.gov) and *Literature Online* (http://lion.chadwyck.com). Purchase of books is possible at on-line booksellers, the largest of which are *Amazon.com* (http://www.amazon.com) and *Barnesandnoble.com* (http://www.barnesandnoble.com).

Teachers often find newspapers and magazines appropriate sources of reading material for their students. Many publishers around the world now post their newspapers and magazines on-line, thereby making access a very simple matter for teachers and students with Internet connections. Numerous lists of on-line periodicals exist on the Web, including *Newspapers Online* (http://www.newspapers.com). Among the major English language periodicals with on-line editions are *The Times* (http://www.the-times.co.uk), *The New York Times* (http://www.nytimes.com), *The Washington Post* (http://www.washingtonpost.com), *The Wall Street Journal* (http://www.wsj.com), *The Christian Science*

Monitor (http://www.csmonitor.com), *The Sydney Morning Herald* (http://www.smh.com.au), *Time* (http://www.time.com), and *Newsweek* (http://www.newsweek.com). Two of the most popular news Web sites for the public as well as for teachers and learners of English are *CNN.com* (http://www.cnn.com) and *BBC Online* (http://www.bbc.co.uk).

Some of these media sites have special sections for teachers and learners, with sample lessons based on materials they publish. Examples are *The New York Times Learning Network* (2000, http://www.nytimes.com/learning); *BBC Schools Online* (2000, http://www.bbc.co.uk/education/schools); and the *Learning Resources* (2000, http://literacynet.org/cnnsf), developed jointly by CNN San Francisco and the Western/Pacific Literacy Network.

Web sites created by museums are potential sources of content for English language classes. *World Wide Arts Resources* (http://wwar.com) is a valuable source of information on Web sites for art and art museums around the world. Popular sites include those of the Louvre in Paris, France (http://www.louvre.fr); the Uffizi Gallery in Florence, Italy (http://www.uffizi.firenze.it); and the National Gallery of Art in the United States (http://www.nga.gov). Science museums can be useful resources as well; see, for example, the excellent educational Web site of the Franklin Institute Science Museum in Philadelphia, in the United States (http://sln.fi.edu).

Finally, no discussion of media Web sites would be complete without an introduction to the *Internet Movie Database* (http://www.imdb.com). This searchable database of almost every movie ever made includes information on casts and plots plus critical reviews. See Figure 5 for a sample reading assignment involving this popular resource.

PROFESSIONAL ORGANIZATIONS AND ASSOCIATIONS

The majority of international professional organizations now have their own Web sites, which makes it possible for members to maintain frequent contact with the organizations. English language teachers can find their own professional organizations on the Web, such as TESOL (http://www.tesol.org), the International Association of Teachers of English as a Foreign Language (IATEFL, http://www.iatefl.org), the Japan Association for Language Teaching (JALT, http://www.jalt.org), and NAFSA: Association of International Educators (http://www.nafsa.org). Also on the Web are organizations of related interest, such as the National Council of Teachers of English (http://www.ncte.org), the American Association for Applied Linguistics (http://www.aaal.org), the Linguistic Society of America (http://www.lsadc.org), and the American Council on the Teaching of Foreign Languages (http://www.actfl.org).

Two organizations devoted to technological issues in teaching are the Computer Assisted Language Instruction Consortium (CALICO, http://www.calico.org) and the Alliance for Computers and Writing (http://english.ttu.edu /acw).

**Figure 5. Sample Assignment Using the *Internet Movie Database*
(http://www.imdb.com)**

EFL 40-10

Independent Web Reading Assignment #5

Your Favorite Movie

1. Go to the *Internet Movie Database* (http://us.imdb.com).
2. Search for material on your favorite film.
3. Read the material and answer the following questions:
   - Who is the film's leading actor?
   - Who is the film's leading actress?
   - Who is the film's director?
   - What is the date of the film?
   - Are there any reviews of this film?
   - If so, are they positive or negative? Explain.
   - Did this film win any Academy Awards?
   - If so, which one(s)?
4. Hand in your answers to these questions along with printouts of the relevant Web pages.

Assignment due date: March 22

Some membership organizations post all or part of their newsletters on-line. *TESOL Matters'* column "Wandering the Web" (Meloni, 2000, http://www .tesol.org/pubs/magz/wanweb.html) contains many Internet links, and its presence on the Web greatly simplifies the process of checking out the sites. JALT's site (http://www.jalt.org) also contains numerous links to the newsletters published by its interest sections.

Associations found on-line that are of particular interest to language teachers are the Center for Applied Linguistics (CAL, http://www.cal.org), which operates the ERIC Clearinghouse on Languages and Linguistics (http:// www.cal.org/ericcll), as well as the National Clearinghouse on Bilingual Education (http://www.ncbe.gwu.edu) and the National Foreign Language Resource Center (http://www.lll.hawaii.edu/nflrc).

ON-LINE WORKSHOPS AND CONFERENCES

TESOL sponsors regular on-line professional development workshops (see *TESOL On-Line Workshops for ESOL Professionals*, 1999, http://www.tesol.org /edprg/1999/olw.html). These workshops last approximately 1 month and give participants an opportunity to interact intensively with other teachers around the world under the guidance of TESOL experts on topics such as task-based learning and CALL. The Teaching in the Community Colleges Online Conference (http://leahi.kcc.hawaii.edu/org/tcon2000), sponsored by the Teaching in the Community Colleges e-mail list and Kapiʻolani Community College in Hawaiʻi, is an annual on-line conference with some 50 presenters on a wide range of topics.

In these workshops and conferences, conference participants and presenters communicate through e-mail lists, Web boards, Web-based chat rooms, or MOOs. Papers written for the conference are posted on the conference's Web site for participants to look over, read, and print, if they desire. Real-time chat sessions with participants are scheduled in chat rooms or MOOs.

In some cases, the conference itself is not held on-line, but the proceedings are made available on the Web. For example, the Consortium of Universities of the Washington Metropolitan Area has posted the proceedings of a symposium it sponsored, *E-Mail, the Web, and MOOs* (Meloni & Miller, 1997, http://gwis .circ.gwu.edu/~washweb/proceedings.html).

ENGLISH LANGUAGE PROGRAMS AND STAFF

University English language programs often have Web pages that offer information of interest not only to potential students of that university but also to English language professionals. A comprehensive list of links to English language programs throughout the world can be found in the *ESL Web Guide* (Sperling, 1999, http://www.eslcafe.com/search) under the heading "Schools."

Faculty in various disciplines often create Web pages to exchange information about their special area of interest. At the *NETEACH-L* Web page (Moody, n.d., http://www.ilc.cuhk.edu.hk/english/neteach/main.html), for instance, you will find a list of links to the home pages of teachers who use the Internet for English teaching.

PUBLISHERS

Major publishers of English language teaching materials post catalogues of their publications on their Web sites. A few publishers go beyond merely displaying their wares and offer some special features to assist teachers in their professional lives. For example, *Longman ELT Connection* (http://www.awl-elt.com) features reviews of recently published books; a calendar of conferences and author talks; and downloadable activities, worksheets, and teachers' tips. Oxford University Press's site (http://www.oup.co.uk) includes a monthly on-line magazine called *ELT Spectrum* (http://www1.oup.co.uk/cite/oup/elt/magazine). Each issue includes "Tips for Teachers," "Grammar Forum," "Author Talk," "Teacher Profile," downloadable worksheets and activities, and a feature article.

LANGUAGE REFERENCE MATERIAL

You and your students may find many useful language reference tools on the Web. *A Web of On-Line Dictionaries* (Beard, 1996, http://www.facstaff.bucknell

.edu/rbeard/diction.html) is a compendium of links to more than 800 dictionaries in more than 160 languages. The many English language dictionaries on-line include *WWWebster Dictionary* (2000, http://www.m-w.com/netdict.htm) and *Collins Cobuild Student's Dictionary Online* (http://springbank.linguistics.ruhr-uni-bochum.de/ccsd). When a word is typed in at the *Newbury House Online Dictionary* (http://nhd.heinle.com), its definition and a sample sentence appear, often accompanied by a photo from the site's 50,000-photo on-line database. There are also specialized English dictionaries, such as the illustrated *Webopedia: Online Computer Dictionary for Internet Terms and Technical Support* (http://webopaedia.com).

Teachers and advanced students will want to refer to *Collins CobuildDirect*, an on-line service for accessing a 50-million-word English corpus made up of actual uses of spoken and written English gathered over the years (see *CobuildDirect Information*, 1999, http://titania.cobuild.collins.co.uk/direct_info.html). You can search the corpus on the Web using Cobuild's free trial on-line concordancer. The search results show how selected words, collocations, or phrases are used in authentic English language contexts, and you can incorporate the examples found into grammar or vocabulary exercises (see the discussion in Tribble & Jones, 1990). English language classes can also use the entire Web as a corpus for lexical and grammatical analysis; see *Grammar Safari* (Mills & Salzmann, 1999, http://deil.lang.uiuc.edu/web.pages/grammarsafari.html) for suggestions along this line.

Purdue University's *Online Writing Lab* (http://owl.english.purdue.edu) has more than 130 instructional handouts, including many on writing and grammar points that are difficult for students of English, such as the use of articles and prepositions. Figure 6 shows a self-access exercise developed by an ESL teacher making use of an *Online Writing Lab* handout.

Numerous other general reference tools are found on the Web. A collection of some very helpful tools can be found at *Research-It!* (http://www.itools.com/research-it).

DOWNLOADABLE SOFTWARE TOOLS

Many free, downloadable software tools can help you make full use of the Web, both for surfing and for creating Web pages (see Figure 7 for tips on avoiding computer viruses when downloading files). *Shareware.com* (http://www.shareware.com) is one comprehensive site for finding software. The column "Daily Double Download" (Gralla, 2000, http://www.zdnet.com/yil/content/depts/doubledl/dlcurrent/dlcurrent.html) also provides information on software that is available for downloading, with two new products featured every day.

Some of the most important downloads are software for listening to audio files and viewing video files (e.g., RealPlayer, 1999; see http://www.real.com), and for deciphering pages in particular formats (e.g., Adobe Acrobat Reader,

Figure 6. Sample Exercise Using a Handout From *Online Writing Lab* (http://owl.English.purdue.edu)

EFL 49

Independent Writing Assignment #2

Paraphrasing Practice

Instructions:

1. Go to Purdue University's *Online Writing Lab* (http://owl.English.purdue.edu).
2. Find the section entitled "Resources for Writers" and the subsection "OWL Handouts."
3. Choose the Paraphrasing handout.
4. Read the Paraphrasing handout. Print it out for future reference.
5. Print out the exercises entitled "Practice Exercises in Paraphrasing."
6. Complete the exercises.
7. After completing the paraphrases, print out the page entitled "Practice in Paraphrasing: Possible Exercise Answers."
8. Compare your paraphrases to the suggested responses.
9. Hand in your paraphrases along with the printout of the possible answers.

Assignment due date: April 12

1999; see http://www.adobe.com/products/acrobat/readstep.html). There are tools for designing Web pages that are almost as easy to use as a word processor is (e.g., Netscape Composer, a component of Netscape Communicator, 1999; see http://home.netscape.com/computing/download), that give Web designers great artistic capabilities (e.g., Paint Shop Pro, 1999; see http://www.jasc.com), and that facilitate the creation of on-line quizzes (e.g., Hot Potatoes, 1999, see http://Web.uvic.ca/hrd/halfbaked; *Ed Tech Tools,* http://motted.hawaii.edu). *CELIA at La Trobe University* (see Holliday, n.d., http://www.latrobe.edu.au /www/education/celia/celia.html) allows users to download free software for language learning and teaching.

Finally, Teleport Pro (1997; see http://www.tenmax.com/teleport/pro) and WebWhacker (1999; see http://www.bluesquirrel.com/products/whacker /whacker.html) are useful software products for downloading Web sites and saving them on a computer disk. Using these products, you can download sites and use them later in classrooms or meeting rooms where no live Internet connection exists.

SITES FOR ENGLISH LANGUAGE LEARNING

Of the many sites especially developed for teachers and learners of English, perhaps the best known is *Dave's ESL Cafe* (http://eslcafe.com). This site includes

Figure 7. Viruses

When downloading files or software from the Internet, it is necessary to take some basic precautions to avoid computer viruses. A computer virus is a malicious piece of programming code that enters your computer software or operating system from an infected file. Computer viruses can cause loss of your data or destruction of your hardware. It is better to use basic safety measures than to lose weeks or months of work.

Computer viruses can enter your system only when you open formatted documents (e.g., word-processing files) or run executable programs (e.g., .exe files using the Microsoft Windows operating system or any other software). A virus cannot infect your system from an e-mail message you have received unless your e-mail software is set up to automatically open attachments that come with the message. Take the following steps to prevent your computer from being infected by a virus:

- Do not open up attachments that come with e-mail messages unless the attachment is something that you have requested or are expecting.
- Download software only from reputable sites. Do not use pirated software.
- Do not use documents or software from other people's diskettes unless you have antivirus software on your computer and it is running.
- Buy good virus protection software from a company such as McAfee (http://www.mcafee.com), Dr. Solomon's Software (http://www.drsolomon.com), or Symantec Corporation (http://www.symantec.com), and install it on your computer. This software can be purchased over the Web or at a computer store.
- Go back to the antivirus software company's Internet site and download upgrades at least monthly. New viruses are introduced frequently, and if you don't upgrade your software, it won't protect your computer.
- If you receive a message about a virus, don't pass the message on unless you first confirm information about it from a reputable computer company or virus protection software company. Most of the messages that are circulated about viruses are actually virus hoaxes (see *SARC Online Virus and Hoax Encyclopedia*, 2000, http://www.symantec.com/avcenter/vinfodb.html).

discussion forums and chat rooms for teachers and students plus many other features, such as a job center, an ESL bookstore, and a collection of quizzes. Other sites containing English language resources include *Linguistic Funland* (http://www.linguistic-funland.com), *Karin's ESL PartyLand* (http://www.eslpartyland.com), and *Tower of English* (http://members.tripod.com/~towerofenglish). The latter offers a daily tip sheet, sent out by e-mail to interested teachers or students of English, that offers suggestions on Web sites to visit. Two comprehensive sites that point to English language resources available on the Web are *The Internet TESL Journal* (http://www.aitech.ac.jp/~iteslj) and

Kenji Kitao's Home Page (http://202.23.150.181/users/kkitao). More than 100 sites for English language learners are linked together in the Web ring *ESLoop* (http://www.tesol.net/esloop).

Several English language learning sites have listening exercises to use with students. *Randall's ESL Cyber Listening Lab* (http://www.esl-lab.com) features more than 100 conversations and lectures to listen to, accompanied by interactive multiple-choice quizzes that provide instant feedback. *English Listening Lounge* (http://www.englishlistening.com) has a number of listening passages from beginning to advanced levels based on ordinary people discussing their lives. *Interactive Listening Comprehension Practice* (Mills, 1999, http://deil .lang.uiuc.edu/lcra) includes authentic passages from National Public Radio and Cable News Network accompanied by quizzes.

Students interested in self-study can be directed to *The ESL Study Hall* (http://gwis2.circ.gwu.edu/~gwvcusas), where they will find annotated links to a number of sites organized by skill area (e.g., reading, writing, vocabulary, grammar, listening, discussion). *The ESL Study Hall* also allows students to write reviews of their favorite *Study Hall* sites and to post the reviews for the benefit of teachers and other students.

Conclusion

The Internet contains numerous resources of interest to educators, especially English language teachers. It can also be a helpful tool for collaboration among teachers, whether in the same city or across the world from each other. We hope that you will not only access the Internet for its resources but also contribute your own materials, knowledge, and ideas via e-mail and the World Wide Web.

Chapter 3

Student Communication and Collaboration

In this chapter, we introduce ways to use the Internet for communication, and for collaborative projects with students in a single class or across classes in different parts of the world.

Computer-assisted language learning was a relatively specialized field in the 1970s and 1980s, attracting the attention of a small number of educators with a particular interest in computers. In the 1990s, though, with the popularization of the Internet, the use of computers in language teaching expanded by leaps and bounds. For the first time, learners of the English language could practice the language 24 hours a day with native speakers or other learners around the world.

Today, the significance of computer-mediated communication in society and the classroom is even greater. Some 3.4 trillion e-mail messages were sent in the United States alone in 1998, or more than 10,000 for every man, woman, and child in the country ("eMarketer Tallies the Number of E-Mail Messages," 1999). E-mail is also becoming a major form of business communication. In fact, in one survey of U.S. business managers, e-mail actually ranked higher than telephone communication or even face-to-face communication as a frequent means of workplace interaction (*E-Mail Tops Telephone*, 1998). With e-mail becoming a principal form of communication for business, academic, and civic affairs, learning how to communicate and collaborate well in this medium must become a goal in its own right.

This chapter introduces a wide range of ways to use e-mail and computer-mediated communication in the classroom. We discuss the use of on-line communication (a) within a single class—between a teacher and individual students, and among the members of a single class—and (b) in long-distance interaction—between students and miscellaneous international contacts, and among two or more classes organized in formal partnerships.

Interaction Within a Single Class

TEACHER-STUDENT INTERACTION

Because of large classes and curricular activities, teachers and individual students often have insufficient opportunities to communicate in the classroom. Likewise, students and teachers may not communicate outside class because of a lack of suitable office hours, busy schedules, or simply shyness on the part of students. E-mail can open up an extra channel for teacher-student communication. Teachers who use e-mail with students need to be aware, however, of the time commitment it may involve. Many students who might hesitate to ask questions in person are much more forthright via e-mail. Over time, you will gain experience in deciding when to give a full reply over e-mail and when to simply acknowledge the concern and save it to discuss at the next class meeting.

The following are some recommended types of teacher-student communication.

Consultation

E-mail is useful for informal consultation. If you let students know that you are willing to communicate with them via e-mail, they will have excellent opportunities for authentic communication. Students may have minor questions that they would hesitate to bother you with in person but for which an e-mail message seems to be an appropriate way to obtain the answer. Figure 1 shows one of the many types of e-mail messages teachers receive from students. Students also e-mail teachers to set up appointments, let teachers know why they've been absent, inquire about assignments, or submit their homework.

Sometimes opportunities for informal consultation facilitate more in-depth communication with students about their language learning strategies or their choices for personal and professional development. Figure 2 shows an e-mail message received from a teacher in an intensive English program at the University of Hawai'i (see Warschauer, 1999, p. 50). The teacher responded with some thoughtful suggestions and comments that helped the writer, a new MA student from Japan, better understand the value of professional networking in the United States.

Figure 1. An E-Mail Message From a Student to a Teacher

```
Date Sent: Sunday, December 05, 1999 5:00 PM
From:      Jean Chen
To:        meloni
Subject:   Q?

About my long research paper, you mark "lack of
outline/table of contents" ...

I do not understand that. Does that mean I have to
add an index in my long research paper? Please answer
me, thanks.
```

Finally, in some cases you may want to make yourself available on-line during office hours for students who, for reasons of geography or mobility, are not able to drop in. You can do this via e-mail or, for real-time communication, with software such as ICQ (1999; see http://www.icq.com) or with a World Wide Web–based chat service (e.g., *Talk City*, http://www.talkcity.com).

Figure 2. A Student Asks for Advice via E-Mail

```
Date:      Mon, 21 Oct 1996 12:38:23 -1000
From:      Miyako <miyako@hawaii.edu>
To:        Luz <luz@hawaii.edu>
Subject:   Today's discussion

I have one more question. Creating professional
network sounds very strange for me because I don't
want to go to Ph.D and I just want to get MA Degree.
I would like to create good relationship to my
academic adviser and the other professors who in my
department through the lecture. I would like to learn
a lot of things from them. I thought it is enough to
study here. I have not ever imagined to create
network byong my department or this university. What
do you think my opinion? Maybe I don't know how
important the academic/professional network mean.

thank you for your time, Luz. :)

Miyako
```

Dialogue Journals

You can extend the benefits of informal teacher-student consultation through a more systematic exchange. A popular technique for this is the teacher-student dialogue journal (Peyton & Reed, 1990). Students turn in a weekly diary to you; you respond with individual comments, questions, and answers.

Though paper dialogue journals have their benefits, they also present logistical difficulties. Because they are usually all collected on the same day, you must bring a mound of journals home to read and answer. Meanwhile, the students have lost access to their journals while you are reading them.

Many teachers have found that electronic dialogue journals achieve the same benefits as or greater benefits than paper journals do, with more convenience and spontaneity. Students can easily send in their journals at any time of day or night, and you can respond at your convenience as well. A good electronic management system on both ends will allow you and your students to keep excellent, searchable records of the correspondence. Wang (1993), in fact, found in research on the differences between the discourse in dialogue journals written on paper and those sent via e-mail that students using e-mail wrote more text, asked more questions, and used more language functions more frequently than students writing on paper did.

Writing Conferences

Modern theories of writing instruction emphasize the importance of writing as a process, not just as the creation of a project. A good writing process involves multiple opportunities to plan, discuss, and revise writing, with the teacher playing the role of an interested and informed reader rather than a judge.

Once again, electronic communication can assist this process. You can use e-mail with students to help them choose a topic or explore their ideas. You can also receive drafts of student papers over e-mail and review and discuss these drafts (see the discussion in Gurevich, 1995). Holding writing conferences by e-mail allows more frequent exchanges, especially if a class meets only once or twice a week, and it provides a convenient written record of all drafts and communications.

Conferencing electronically about writing has advantages and disadvantages. Face-to-face communication allows the rapid back-and-forth that promotes fruitful and in-depth exploration. Electronic communication can be excellent for commenting on a few specific points in a medium that will be accessible to the student for postanalysis. Schultz (2000), in a study comparing face-to-face and electronic conferencing for learners of French, found that students incorporated more specific changes in response to electronic feedback but often made more global changes following in-depth, face-to-face discussion.

CLASS INTERACTION

One disadvantage of a teacher-student e-mail exchange is the amount of time it takes the teacher. Intense individual e-mail exchanges with many students may be too much for some teachers to handle. By focusing instead on setting up electronic communication among students, you can minimize this disadvantage while providing a valuable opportunity for peer interaction.

Most of the means of communication noted above between a teacher and one student can be extended to broader classroom interaction between the teacher and many students simultaneously or among the students themselves. You can handle the mechanics of class interaction in several ways. First, you may want to create a Web site for the class. (See Supplement: How to Make Web Pages for information.) This site can be a focal point for obtaining information and a branching-off point for other forms of discussion through e-mail or Web boards. For example, Janice Cook's home page for her ESL writing class includes links to the syllabus, background resources, the library, and an e-mail discussion list (see Figure 3).

Interaction among students and the teacher can be organized in a number of ways. First, many universities and school districts have the capacity to establish e-mail lists. If your university or school does not have this capacity, you can

Figure 3. Home Page for an ESL Writing Class (Cook, n.d.)

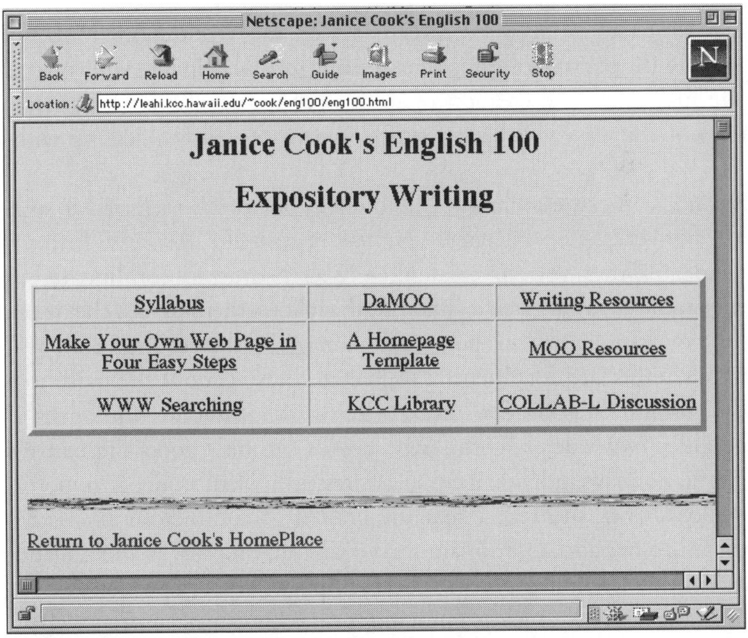

Figure 4. Creating Your Own E-Mail List

Any teacher can create an e-mail discussion list at a Web site such as *eGroups.com* (http://www.egroups.com). In setting up the list, you will have a number of options to consider:

- *management:* Will you manage the list yourself, or will you invite a student or another teacher to be a comanager?
- *subscription:* Will the managers enter the members' names, or will the members subscribe themselves—and if they do subscribe themselves, will all new subscriptions need a manager's approval?
- *welcome message:* Will a welcome message be sent to all new members? If so, what will it say?
- *posting:* Will only the managers be able to post messages, or will any member be able to post messages? If any member can post, will the messages first have to be approved by a manager?
- *publicity:* Will the list be hidden (i.e., available only to invited members), or will members of the public be able to find out about it and join?
- *list of members:* Can participants see the e-mail addresses of all members, or can only the managers see them?
- *replies:* Will replies to messages by default go to the entire list or only back to the writer of the message?

establish a list free of charge at several sites on the World Wide Web, such as *eGroups.com* (http://www.egroups.com; see Figure 4). Finally, your own e-mail software may allow the creation of simple group lists. Once a list is created, members of the class will have a simple means of communicating with each other.

Second, you can establish a Web bulletin board (also referred to as a *Web board*). For example, Nicenet's *Internet Classroom Assistant* (http://www.nicenet.org) allows you to create free Web boards for on-line discussion. Students in the class are given a password that allows them to join the discussion. You or your students can post and manage a shared list, participate in discussions, and share documents. (To look at ready-made Web boards to use in classes, consult the *Forum One Index,* http://www.forumone.com, or the *Delphi Forums,* http://www.delphi.com.) Web boards can be a good alternative when students do not have individual e-mail addresses or when students' opportunities to download, save, and read e-mail are limited. A commercial alternative to a Web board, especially appropriate for writing classrooms, is the collaborative writing software CommonSpace (1999; see http://www.sixthfloor.com/CS1.html), which allows students to leave annotations on each others' written work.

Finally, there are several ways to organize real-time discussion in class among groups of students, ranging from the commercial software Daedalus InterChange (a component of Daedalus Integrated Writing Environment, 1997; see http://www.daedalus.com), to MOOs for students of English, such as *schMOOze University* (http://schmooze.hunter.cuny.edu:8888), to chat rooms set up at Internet sites such as *Talk City* (http://www.talkcity.com).

Once the means have been established, electronic communication among the members of a class can take place in class or outside class.

In-Class Discussion

Classes that have access to a computer laboratory and to real-time conferencing software, such as Daedalus InterChange (or any chat software on the Internet), can meet occasionally for computer-assisted written conversation. In written conversation, students type all their comments onto an individual screen, and the comments immediately appear on the screens of the other students. Written conversation is especially valuable in writing classes because it gives the students much more time on task to gain written fluency. Indeed, many writing teachers (of ESL and of English composition) use written conversation on a daily basis. If you teach general language classes, you will probably want to use it only occasionally in order not to supplant oral communication activities. Nevertheless, even in general language classes, written conversation has several advantages:

- All students can "speak" at once, giving shy students a greater chance to participate (Kern, 1995a; Warschauer, 1996a).
- Students can notice, refer to, save, and reuse input, which allows them to assimilate vocabulary, collocations, and grammar (Warschauer, 1999).
- Students have greater control over the planning time for their output, which allows them to reach for more complex terms (Warschauer, 1996a).

To what extent these benefits are achieved will probably rely somewhat on the software chosen. For example, the interface of much chat software encourages very short snippets of communication (thus encouraging fluency more than complexity) whereas the interface of Daedalus InterChange encourages students to write in longer sentences or paragraphs.

Out-of-Class Discussion

A more frequent use of electronic communication for the language classroom is out-of-class discussion. The electronic forum gives students opportunities for language practice and communication that extend beyond the limited class time.

For example, a reading and writing class might hold part of its class discussion on-line using an e-mail list or Web board. You could ask students to prepare discussion questions about their reading assignments, post them for others to see, and post responses to a certain number of the questions posed by other students. Or you might ask students to form small groups for electronic discussion on a particular topic or in preparation for a presentation. Students can also exchange and comment on drafts of their writing electronically.

Janda (1995) has created a series of activities that encourage collaborative communication and writing via e-mail. In these activities, students work in groups to introduce themselves, discuss films and literature, discuss a series of controversial beliefs, analyze graphs and charts for a class partner, explain humor in comics to a partner, solve a literary puzzle, and prepare for an oral presentation. Other communicative e-mail activities include the creation of chain stories (with one student writing after the other; see Manteghi, 1995) or of collaborative mysteries in which different students write the beginning, middle, and end of the stories (Opp-Beckman, 1997).

There is no limit to the ways of using various forms of electronic discussion to enhance a language classroom. The general suggestions below will help you make the best use of such discussion.

- Remember that electronic discussion takes planning and organization. Don't assume that students will make good use of an electronic space simply by its being opened.

- During most activities, play an active but not dominant role. In a whole-class discussion, think of some good questions to get the discussion rolling, and then jump in to add value at appropriate moments. Be prepared, though, for the dynamics to be less controlled than in an oral discussion with the teacher planted firmly at the center of the room.

- Think carefully about integrating electronic discussion with other classroom activities. Electronic discussion can be an excellent follow-up to or preparation for an oral discussion on the same activity (Kern, 1995b; Kroonenberg, 1995). It can also be a good way for groups of students to prepare their work on a project.

- Avoid direct correction of students' errors in electronic discussion. Rather, model correct language for them in your responses. Also, analyze the transcripts to gain information about the students' language level and needs. You may want to prepare lessons based on some of the linguistic features noted in the students' written communication or even have the students work in groups to analyze linguistic features of their writing (Kelm, 1995).

Long-Distance Communication

Long-distance communication and collaboration present even more opportunities for the language classroom. In this section we discuss (a) at-large, long distance communication, which involves communication with miscellaneous partners rather than exchanges between classes, and (b) formal multiclass partnerships.

AT-LARGE, LONG-DISTANCE COMMUNICATION

Keypals

Keyboard pen pals, or *keypals*, correspond with each other via e-mail. Keypal exchanges can provide motivational benefits for beginning- and intermediate-level learners, who get satisfaction from using their new language in authentic communication. Learners at all levels can benefit from keypal exchanges if these exchanges have enough structure to keep the students interested and active. However, keypal exchanges designed without a specific purpose or task may lose their appeal and benefits over time.

Keypals can be found in partner classes or on Web sites where individuals sign up for partners. You and your students should decide whether you prefer other English learners or native speakers as keypals. Some places to start looking are listed below.

- *E-Pals* (http://www.britcoun.org.hk/epals/epals_new.html) offers individual pen pals from around the world.
- *Englishtown* (http://www.englishtown.com) has a keypal club for individual English learners.
- *Keypal Opportunities for Students* (Kitao & Kitao, 1999a, http://ilc2 .doshisha.ac.jp/users/kkitao/online/www/keypal.htm) is a complete listing of keypal resources.
- At *KeyPals Club* (http://www.mightymedia.com/keypals), students can find and correspond with individual keypals from around the world.
- *Linguistic Funland* (http://www.linguistic-funland.com) lists ESL teachers looking for pen pals.
- *Tower of English* (http://members.tripod.com/~towerofenglish) lists individual English learner keypals.

In organizing keypal exchanges, keep in mind that not all keypals are equally responsive. It can be quite disappointing when a few students in a class haven't received replies from their keypals. Students should thus correspond with more than one keypal to increase the chance that communication will be ongoing (Robb, 1996; Shetzer, 1997). Another way to compensate for individual dropout is to have people communicate in small groups rather than one-to-one.

Expert Interviews

Expert interviews are similar to keypal exchanges, but they take place between learners of English and people who are chosen for their degree of expertise. They may be informants on cultural issues (e.g., native speakers of English or residents of a particular country, region, or state under examination) or experts in a topical area (e.g., related to science, literature, or business). Experts can be located by you or, in high-intermediate or advanced classes, by the students. You can supply the topics for the interviews, or the students can develop them. Interviews and discussion can be held on an ongoing basis or during a single on-line appearance via a Web board or a chat room.

For example, a teacher of high school students in Paris who are interested in space shuttles could invite a scientist at the National Air and Space Museum in Washington, DC, to meet them in a chat room for a question-and-answer session. A teacher of elementary school students in Minneapolis who want to learn about minority groups in their community could ask a local government official to respond to students' questions on an electronic bulletin board. Students in Tokyo, Japan, who are studying about Australia might want to carry out a series of interviews with students in Sydney, Australia. If possible, you can structure such contacts into a larger set of activities that includes preliminary instruction in the types of language functions the students will need to conduct the interviews and postinterview assignments in which students actively use the information gathered.

Surveys

Another way to provide more structure in e-mail writing is through the planning and implementation of surveys (Ady, 1995; Kendall, 1995). You or your students can locate informants in different parts of the world through keypal sources, through chat rooms and discussion forms on the World Wide Web, or through your own contacts. Students can then work in groups to design surveys to conduct via e-mail. After conducting the surveys, the students tabulate the results and present them to their classmates in written or oral presentations.

International Group Discussion

You may want your students to have the chance to participate in group discussions with other English learners from around the world. The numerous forums for this include the following:

- *ESL Discussion Center* (Sperling, 2000, http://www.eslcafe.com /discussion), a forum for asynchronous and real-time discussion on topics such as computers, culture, health and fitness, science, and sports (see Figure 5)
- *schMOOze University* (http://schmooze.hunter.cuny.edu:8888), a MOO for real-time discussion and simulation among English teachers and students around the world

**Figure 5. Discussion Forums at *Dave's ESL Cafe's*
ESL Discussion Center (Sperling, 2000)**

Cinema	Health and Fitness	Opinions
Computers	Hobbies	Pets
Culture	Holidays	Science
Current News	Learning English	Sports
English Schools	Literature	The Strange and Mysterious
Family	Making Friends	TOEFL
Food	Music	Travel

- the *SL-Lists* (Holliday & Robb, n.d., http://www.latrobe.edu.au/www
  /education/sl/sl.html), a series of 10 e-mail discussion lists for students
  around the world, organized by topic (e.g., business, music) and level
  (e.g., general discussion lists for beginning- and advanced-level students)

Some students will likely become addicted to these or other international discussion sites and spend a great deal of time communicating there. Others will become bored quickly. Either group, though, will most likely benefit from structured activities that help establish communicative goals or tasks. You can ask students to conduct interviews or surveys, post a minimal number of messages and report back on them, or otherwise participate in discussions in a way that feeds into class objectives.

The types of international communication you involve your students in will depend a great deal on the level, age, and goals of your students. More advanced students, such as those at the undergraduate or graduate level, need to learn how to participate in international communication for professional and academic networking. For example, graduate students in an intensive English program at the University of Hawai'i were required to find and join an e-mail discussion list related to their own professional interests and were taught strategies for using e-mail to network effectively in their fields (Warschauer, 1999). In this sense, electronic communication becomes more than a vehicle for practicing general English. For the students, it is a means for mastering the kinds of professional communication required of them.

INTERCLASS PROJECTS

Interclass projects involve two or more classes from different parts of the world working together via the Internet toward common goals and objectives. Usually, planning and implementing interclass projects requires a great deal of time and energy, and in some cases these projects achieve disappointing results because of logistical or coordination difficulties. Yet, when long-distance interclass projects are well organized among like-minded partners, the results can open up students' lives to forms of international collaboration, communication, action, and learning that they may have never experienced before.

Interclass projects usually involve five stages: (a) planning, (b) contact, (c) investigation, (d) finale, and (e) evaluation.

Planning

The many logistical and pedagogical challenges in organizing an interclass project make careful planning essential. After having worked together on several interclass Internet projects, Corio and Meloni have developed the following guidelines to take into consideration when choosing partners and launching an Internet interclass project:

- *students' level:* The two or more groups of English learners brought together for a project should be at approximately the same level of English language proficiency.
- *schedule:* The class schedules of the participating classes, including their vacation schedules, should match as closely as possible.
- *objectives:* If possible, the course objectives should be similar. If one course is a writing course and the other is a conversation course, devising a joint project is difficult though not impossible. (In such a situation, the students could work together but complete different final products; e.g., a written paper for one and an oral presentation for the other.)
- *teacher commitment and philosophy:* The teaching partners should share a strong degree of commitment to the project and, if possible, a similar philosophy of or approach to English teaching.
- *core project:* The collaborative project should be an integral part of the course and not an extra activity so that the students see its relevance and accept it more readily. In the same vein, students should be expected to put in a great deal of effort, as their lack of follow-through will affect not only them and their classmates but also their partners in other classes.

This last point was made well by a coordinator of the International Email Classroom Connections program:

> There is a significant difference in educational outcome depending on whether a teacher chooses to incorporate email classroom connections as (1) an ADD-ON process, like one would include a guest speaker, or (2) an INTEGRATED process, in the way one would include a new textbook. The email classroom connection seems sufficiently complex and time consuming that if there are goals beyond merely having each student send a letter to a person at a distant school, the ADD-ON approach can lead to frustration and less-than-expected academic results—the necessary time and resources come from other things that also need to be done. On the other hand, when the email classroom connection processes are truly integrated into the ongoing structure of homework and

student classroom interaction, then the results can be educationally transform-ing. (Roberts, 1994, cited in Warschauer, 1995a, p. 95)

An excellent place to meet potential teaching partners and discuss joint projects is *NETEACH-L* (see Moody, n.d., http://www.ilc.cuhk.edu.hk/english /neteach/main.html), the e-mail discussion list for teachers interested in the Internet and English language teaching.

Contact

Once the partners have been selected and the project planned, the next step is establishing contact among the students. You can use any of the media discussed in this chapter—e-mail lists, Web boards, chat rooms, or videoconferencing—to facilitate contact. And other nonelectronic means should be considered as well. It is often effective to personalize the project by exchanging culture packets (through the postal service) that contain items such as school newspapers, photos, or banners.

In the early stages of a project, students should develop teams (at one site or across sites, depending on the nature of the project) and should be encouraged to engage in friendly introductions. Taking time for some personal communication will humanize the long-distance partners and establish better working relations, not to mention making the project a more enjoyable experience for everyone.

Investigation

The next stage of the project inevitably involves some kind of collaborative inquiry. This might fall into one of the following categories:

- *culture:* Students exchange experiences about their own cultural back-grounds, looking at topics such as oral histories of family members; poetry, folklore, or religion in their community; or religious beliefs and values. For example, Gaer (1995) organized a project in which adult students of English shared folktales with middle school students, who used the folktales to write and illustrate books that they gave back to the adults.
- *literature and film:* Students read the same books or watch the same films. For example, Soh and Soon (1991) organized a project in which English learners in Singapore and in Montreal, Canada, read and discussed stories in English reflecting each group's culture.
- *community:* Students work in teams to investigate and compare social, environmental, political, economic, cultural, or geographic aspects of their communities. For example, Hess (1995, http://www.nyu.edu /pages/hess/cities.html) has organized several "cities projects" in which students from several locations investigated their communities and published detailed electronic guides and videos (see Meloni, 1995, 1997).

- *academic research and writing:* Students form teams according to their academic interests and share notes, resources, drafts, or papers. For example, R. Vilmi (personal communication, May 1999) organized a project involving joint academic research by teams of six to eight students with similar academic backgrounds in several countries. Comparing magazine and newspaper articles on a particular topic from the perspective of 11 different countries was one of the most interesting aspects of the project. In another project, teams of ESL students in Richmond, Virginia, and Washington, DC, formed groups for peer editing of their writing (Corio & Meloni, 1995).

- *simulation:* Teams of students work on simulated solutions to real problems, in the process working together to prepare reports, brochures, curriculum vitae, cover letters, funding proposals, speeches, and other documents. In one elaborate simulation, students in 14 countries worked in teams representing various national delegations and nongovernmental organizations to develop a new draft treaty for a United Nations conference on the Law of the Sea (Mak & Crookall, 1995). They learned writing, negotiation, communication, and language skills as well as many technical skills, such as how to upload and download documents to and from the Internet.

Comparative exploration and investigation is appropriate for students of all ages. In a project organized by K. Eini (personal communication, May 1999), children in Israel and the United States drew monsters and then described them to their partners via e-mail. The partner class redrew the monsters based on the e-mail descriptions. The two sets of drawings were uploaded to the Internet, and the children evaluated them for similarities and differences. In another project (Livesy & Tudoreanu, 1995), elementary school children in Romania and the United States organized field trips to a space center and a planetarium in their two communities and shared their experiences via e-mail. No matter what the age or level of the students is, an inquiry-based project helps focus the communication and develop students' skills in planning, critical thinking, investigation, and analysis.

Finale

Interclass projects should build up to some kind of final product or presentation. This helps guarantee that the students not only develop chatting skills but are strongly encouraged to put all their communication, language, and technical skills toward producing a high-quality package. This product might be a jointly produced video, a printed newspaper, an oral presentation for other classes at their school, a simulated newscast, or a written brochure. In many cases, the final document will be published on-line as a way of sharing it with the partner class and with others around the world. (For a discussion of student publishing, see chapter 5; see Supplement: How to Make Web Pages for information on Web page creation.)

Evaluation

The final stage of an interclass project is evaluation. The nature of such projects, which are based on long-distance collaborative work, necessitates alternative approaches to evaluation. The following are some types of evaluation to consider:

- *portfolios:* Allow the students to submit a portfolio of their work, based on a final product, documents produced along the way, e-mail messages, and other relevant documents.
- *self-assessment:* Have the students evaluate their own work either individually or in groups.
- *contracts:* Have individuals or groups negotiate contracts at the beginning of the process in which they specify their learning objectives and activities. (Fulfillment of contracts is then noted in the portfolio or self-assessment.)

Evaluation of another sort takes place when students on one team judge the work of other teams in order to determine the winner of a simulation or a contest. In such cases, students' work can be presented on the Web for review and evaluation by the other international teams.

Finally, you need to evaluate the overall project. This can be accomplished by analyzing print or on-line texts, surveying or interviewing students, and analyzing classroom processes with the assistance of videotape or observation notes. Including on-line, project-based interclass learning as a central element of language teaching represents a substantial new direction, and interested teachers should document the strengths and weaknesses of their efforts as completely as possible.

Example: US-SiberLink

In the US-SiberLink international collaborative project (Braunstein, Meloni, & Zolotareva, 1999, http://www.gwu.edu/~washweb/us-siberlink.htm), students at two U.S. universities (the University of California, Santa Barbara, and the George Washington University in Washington, DC) and one university in Russia (Yakutsk State University, Yakutsk, Siberia) collaborated on academic and field research. The primary objectives of the project were to (a) provide students with authentic writing and reading opportunities, (b) inform students about a particular content area (the Y2K computer problem), (c) acquaint students with the culture of three diverse cities, and (d) familiarize students with the use of multimedia on the Internet.

The project's multimedia Web site (see Figure 6) served as a virtual course book. The project syllabus was posted on the site along with links to on-line reading assignments. Most of the readings were located on the Web and therefore were listed with active links. The site also featured photos of the faculty and students accompanied by written and audio messages (in RealAudio format) and videos of campus tours and of lectures by a variety of professors (in RealVideo format). The teachers involved created interactive culture and language quizzes using a variety of software, including Dreamweaver (1998; see http:// www.macromedia.com/software/dreamweaver), Hot Potatoes (1999; see http:// Web.uvic.ca/hrd/halfbaked), and a Web page template from *How to Make a Successful ESL/EFL Teacher's Web Page* (Kelly, 1997, http://www.aitech.ac.jp /~iteslj/Articles/Kelly-MakePage). A Web board and a chat room were also available for formal and informal discussion among the participants. The project had four phases:

1. The students learned about each other via photos and brief autobiographies posted to the Web site. They also became familiar with the cultures of the three cities via selected informational Web sites and gained the necessary skills in using e-mail and the Web.

2. The students began to gather general information on a specific content area, potential computer problems related to the advent of the year 2000. They watched and listened to lectures (in RealVideo format) and

Figure 6. Home Page of the US-SiberLink Project (Braunstein, Meloni, & Zolotareva, 1999)

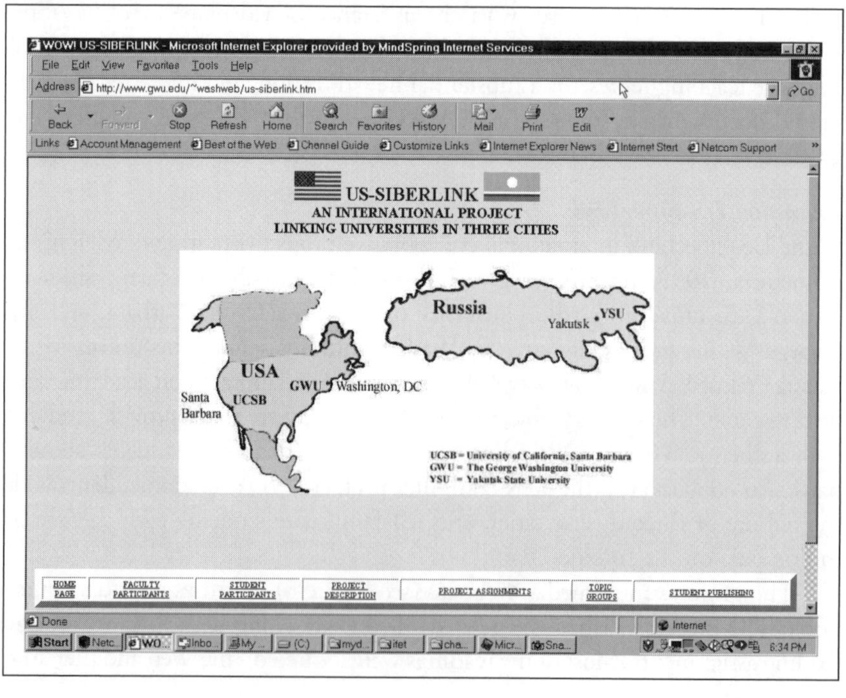

read materials about Y2K for background knowledge (found by clicking the mouse on the URLs in the reading list).

3. The students were divided into *netgroups* (i.e., groups made up of students from each university, who collaborated via the Internet). Each netgroup focused on a different aspect of the Y2K problem (e.g., the impact of Y2K on financial institutions, airlines, private citizens). Members of each group conducted interviews with local residents in their respective cities and exchanged the results via e-mail.

4. Each netgroup prepared a final report. Drafts of the report were exchanged via e-mail, and each group's final report was then posted to the project's Web site. (For a more detailed discussion of this project, see Braunstein, Meloni, & Zolotareva, 2000.)

Conclusion

W. B. Yeats said that "education is not the filling of a pail, but the lighting of a fire." In our experience, there is no better means to light students' fire than to involve them in authentic and challenging communication, inquiry, and problem solving using computers and the Internet. To accomplish this, teachers have to rethink traditional ways of teaching. They must engage in acts of creative imagination and ask their students to do the same. The positive results achieved are sometimes matched by the frustrations of technical problems or the difficulty of trying open-ended tasks in narrowly defined academic time periods. But we believe the process is worthwhile, and necessary, if teachers are to help students achieve their full potential in the age of information technology.

Chapter 4

Student Research

In this chapter, we discuss the nature of student research on the Internet and examine tools and activities for promoting on-line research skills in the English language classroom.

The current era has seen an explosion of information that is unprecedented in human history. Some 2,300 scientific articles are published in the United States alone every day (Tenopir & King, 1997), and the global store of recorded information is said to double every 2 years (Wilson, 1994). We are clearly living in a world where it is no longer sufficient to know what our parents or grandparents knew—or even what we ourselves were taught 5 years ago.

Not only is information growing, but it is also becoming more accessible. The World Wide Web is quickly becoming a massive repository of information—and misinformation—on virtually every topic imaginable.

But information is not knowledge. Indeed, the vast amount of information on the Web can hinder the development of knowledge because that information is so comprehensive and unorganized. Thus the skills of locating, categorizing, and interpreting on-line information are key literacies of the on-line era. Without these new informational literacies, "future citizens will be as disempowered as those who today cannot write, read, or use a library" (Lemke, 1998, p. 290).

And although these literacies are important in any written language, they are of special importance in English, because some 85% of the world's electronic information is said to be in the English language (Crystal, 1997). They thus form an important part of the English language curriculum.

In this chapter, we discuss how to incorporate on-line research into the English language curriculum. First, we review search engines and how to use them. We then discuss strategies for using Web searches in English teaching and describe individual and collaborative research projects in which to employ search tools and strategies.

Search Engines

Many of the on-line resources mentioned in chapter 2, such as virtual libraries, on-line media, and language reference materials, will also be of benefit to students. The most valuable tool for on-line research, however, is the *search engine.* Search engines help you locate information on the Internet in two main ways: through Web crawler technology and through search directories.

Most search engines use a program called a *Web crawler,* which moves through the Internet continuously, reading Web pages and indexing the information available. If you do a search for the phrase "English teaching," for example, the search engine will show you a list of all the pages the crawler has found that include that phrase. Different search engines use different algorithms to determine the order in which the pages are listed (*Google,* http://www .google.com, offers the most sophisticated and helpful method of ordering pages; see below). Some search engines, in addition to crawling and indexing Web pages, have access to additional, private collections of documents not ordinarily found on the Web (see, e.g., *Northern Light,* http://www.northernlight.com, described below). Note, though, that any single search engine crawls through only a minority of the world's Web pages, and even all the search engines taken together do not reach the entire Web. A *metasearch engine* (see *Dogpile,* http:// www.dogpile.com, described below) can be useful in searching a larger number of pages.

In addition to Web crawlers, most search engines use search directories maintained by people who visit Web sites and categorize them into a logical, organized hierarchy. *Yahoo!* (http://yahoo.com) is perhaps the best known search directory. As pictured in Figure 1, when you click on a topic of interest to you at *Yahoo!,* such as education, you are directed to subtopics. Subtopics related to education, for example, are organized by region, culture or group, or subject.

A more impressive directory is the *Open Directory Project* (http://dmoz.org), or *ODP.* The *ODP,* which claims to be the largest human-edited directory of the Web, covers some 1.5 million pages in 250 million distinct categories, assembled

Figure 1. A Search Directory (http://www.yahoo.com)

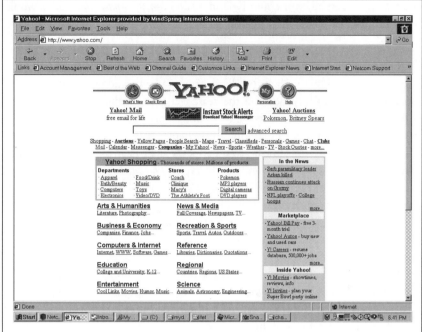

by more than 20,000 volunteer editors (Durham, 2000). The *ODP* is used by a number of popular search engines, including *Google, Netscape Search* (http://search.netscape.com), *Lycos* (http://www.lycos.com), and *HotBot* (http://hotbot.lycos.com).

Search engines can be used in two main ways to find information on the Internet. Perhaps the simplest way—though not necessarily the fastest—is to click down through the listings in a search directory. For example, in the *ODP*, you can click down through the path *Education* → *Subjects* → *English-as-a-Second-Language* → *Student Resources* to find links to *Vocabulary University* (http://www.vocabulary.com) or *The ESL Study Hall* (http://gwis2.circ.gwu.edu /~gwvcusas).

The second and more common way to find information on the Web with a search engine is to type a key word or phrase in the search box and click on "Search." This kind of search is more successful if you use the appropriate syntax, which varies by search engine. In most, you can use quotation marks (" ") for phrases and a minus sign (−) for exclusion. For example, typing *"Mary Smith"* and clicking "Search" will yield a list of pages containing that name, whereas a search for *Mary Smith* (i.e., without the quotation marks) will lead you to pages that include the word *Mary* and the word *Smith* but not necessarily connected to each other. If you are looking for a person named Mary Smith who has nothing to do with basketball, you could type in *"Mary Smith" –basketball*. This would give you a list of pages that include the name *Mary Smith* but not the word *basketball*.

GOOGLE

Launched in 1998 by two Stanford University graduate students, *Google* (http:// google.com) has quickly become the search engine of choice for smart Web surfers. *Google*'s best feature is its page-ranking algorithm, which is based on how many other Internet users are linking to particular pages. As a consequence, the page you are looking for almost always appears at or near the top of the list of search results. As an illustration, if you type *"Harvard University"* and click "Search," the page at the top of the results list will be the university's home page rather than, for example, the page of a former graduate student at Harvard. *Google* even has an "I feel lucky" selection that allows you to go directly to the page at the top of the list without even seeing the search results, a strategy that works more often than not.

Several other features help *Google* rise above the competition. First, unlike other search engines, it allows you to choose between going to a Web page itself or to a cached (saved) version of the page, thus guaranteeing that you will be able to find the information on the page even if it has been deleted or changed. Second, the search engine allows users to conduct full-text searches of pages in a particular category of the *ODP,* which are also intelligently ranked as described above. Finally, *Google* includes very few advertisements or other clutter, so its pages load quickly. For all these reasons, *Google* is especially helpful and easy to use for English language learners, and it is a powerful tool for teachers as well.

ALTAVISTA

AltaVista (http://altavista.com), which indexes a relatively large portion of the Web, is a good alternative if you cannot find what you are looking for on *Google*. A special feature of *AltaVista* is its ability to provide an instantaneous translation of any Web page into several languages. Because the translation is word for word, it is not always highly accurate, but it at least tells roughly what the Web page is about. (For a discussion of this translation feature, see Meloni, 1998b.)

NORTHERN LIGHT

Two features of *Northern Light* (http://northernlight.com) make it an attractive search engine. First, it searches not only the World Wide Web but also 6,200 full-text publications not normally available on the Web. In addition, the search results—including free materials and special collections documents available for a fee—are automatically placed into customized search folders organized by category.

YAHOO!

As a search engine, *Yahoo!* (http://www.yahoo.com) has no distinguishing features other than its own proprietary directory, which is one of the oldest on the Web. What makes *Yahoo!* distinctive is its complete on-line portal. Visitors can sign up for free e-mail accounts, shop on-line, or chat with people who have similar interests. They can also create a personalized version of the search site with their favorite links, customized news, and chat room.

DOGPILE

Dogpile (http://dogpile.com), a metasearch engine, allows you to simultaneously conduct searches through some 30 popular search engines. The results are organized into sections headed by the name of the search engine queried. *Dogpile* and other metasearch engines (e.g., *All-in-One Search Page*, http://www .allonesearch.com) may be helpful in carrying out a highly esoteric search that fails to turn up results in individual search engines.

Classroom Activities and Projects

Knowing what tools and resources are available is a first step, but the most important challenge is learning to use them well. In the rest of this chapter, we discuss activities and projects that incorporate Web-based research into instruction. The activities described here include concept mapping, on-line scavenger hunts, the organization of search results, the exploration of search tools, the evaluation of Web sites, and the incorporation of Web-based searches in independent and collaborative research projects.

CONCEPT MAPPING

The unstructured nature of the Web makes it an easy place to wander aimlessly and "surf" with little direction or purpose. For this reason, you may want to select activities before starting on-line searches to help students sharpen their research focus.

Conducting successful Internet research involves knowing how to make connections between ideas in a nonlinear fashion. One activity that helps build this knowledge is *concept mapping*. Concept maps are visual pictures of topics and subtopics, like the example in Figure 2. You can organize activities that require students to visually explore the associations between their ideas by creating these kinds of concept maps.

The concept map in Figure 2 contains a main topic, Travel, which was broken down into three subtopics, Places to Go, Things to Bring, and Plane Tickets. Each of these subtopics was then broken down into three additional subtopics. We recommend that students incorporate questions, phrases, and other structures into the concept map instead of just listing single words.

Figure 2. Concept Map in Tree Form

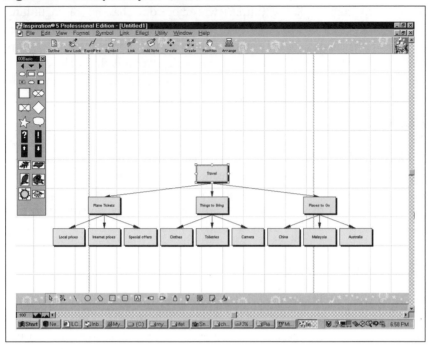

Concept mapping is useful for individual or group brainstorming. It is often helpful to first create a concept map as a class on an overhead transparency, blackboard, or computer projection that you write on while students suggest ideas and connections. To follow this up, you might group students into twos or threes to create concept maps that relate to the class map they have just created. Students could, for example, expand on various nodes of the tree and then share their maps with the class. For individual work, students can work on concept maps related to their own research interests, with your input. This work could be followed up with a homework assignment in which students produce a detailed map.

Concept maps can be done on paper or with computer software, such as Inspiration (1997), which was used to create the graphics in Figures 2 and 3. This software package offers many options, such as viewing the concept map as a traditional linear outline with Roman numerals, as in Figure 3, or as a top-down, bottom-up, or left or right tree structure, as in Figure 2.

Whether students create maps on a computer or ordinary paper, concept mapping can help students focus their research ideas before visiting Web search sites. Students can consult their concept maps for key words to use in search engines, for example.

Figure 3. Concept Map in Outline Form

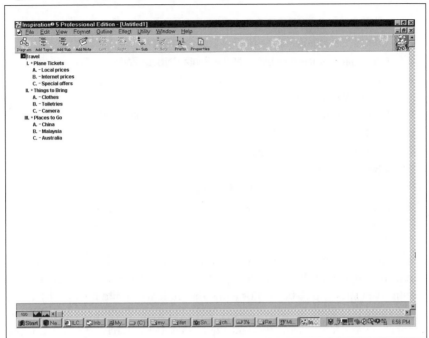

ON-LINE SCAVENGER HUNTS

On-line scavenger hunts are a stimulating way to use search tools in the language classroom. A scavenger hunt is a list of questions that students answer by accessing on-line search tools (see the example in Figure 4). Students search the Web to find answers to the questions.

Scavenger hunts done early in a semester can help students practice Web-searching techniques. At other times hunts can focus on specific content or linguistic material related to the objectives of the course. By having students work in pairs during scavenger hunts, you can encourage oral communication to supplement reading and computer practice. Students can also do scavenger hunts for homework if they have access to a computer and the Internet outside class. Students of all ages often enjoy a competitive scavenger hunt, in which some kind of reward is given to whoever answers all the questions first.

The questions in the scavenger hunt shown in Figure 4 all have specific, limited answers. For a more challenging activity, you can design an open-ended scavenger hunt, in which the questions have more than one possible answer. With large classes, it is advisable to create two or more versions of the scavenger hunt by changing the order of the questions. This will prevent the entire class from going to a single Web site at the same time, which can slow down Internet

Figure 4. Santa Barbara Scavenger Hunt

1. What is the population of Santa Barbara County?
2. What is the address of the Natural Café Restaurant?
3. Name three of the new births at the Santa Barbara Zoo.
4. What TOEFL score is required to enter the chemistry department at the University of California at Santa Barbara?
5. How much does it cost to take a day trip to Anacapa Island?
6. What cities can you fly to from the Santa Barbara Airport?
7. Name three beaches in Santa Barbara.
8. What is Lotusland?
9. Where is the Santa Barbara Public Library?
10. How much does it cost to take a train from Santa Barbara to San Francisco?

access. In designing a scavenger hunt, you also must decide the scope of the search. You may limit the search to a particular on-line newspaper or to a list of specific Web sites (e.g., 10 sites) or allow the students to find answers by using search engines to look anywhere on the Web. For a more advanced activity, you might allow students to write their own questions, perhaps related to a theme the students are discussing in class, and search for the answers together on Web sites.

To find ready-made scavenger hunts, search for them with an Internet search engine. *Internet Scavenger Hunts* (White, 1998, http://home.earthlink.net /~athearn), for example, offers several hunts suitable for third- through sixth-grade students; see also *World Wide Web Scavenger Hunt* (Boone, n.d., http://www.crpc.rice.edu/CRPC/GT/sboone/Lessons/Titles/hunt/hunt.html).

ORGANIZING RESEARCH RESULTS

Once students know how to find information on the Web, they must learn to save and organize it. In this section, we discuss several ways to assist students in learning how to systematically categorize information from the Web.

Paper and Pencil

In one approach to compiling results from Internet searching, you might have students fill out a paper form to turn in to you. This form might ask for three pieces of information on each result: (a) the title of the Web page encountered, (b) the address (URL) of the Web page, and (c) a brief description of the content of the Web page in the student's own words. This approach might work well with students who are not entirely adept at using a computer. One problem with this approach, however, is that students frequently make mistakes in writing down the URL of the Web site.

Bookmarks and Favorites

As an alternative, students can compile their results on a diskette by saving links to Web pages, or *bookmarks,* in a file. The links are called *Bookmarks* in Netscape Communicator (1999) and *Favorites* in Microsoft Internet Explorer (1999). The most effective way to use a Favorites or Bookmarks file is to create a series of folders and subfolders that directly relate to your research interests. In the Favorites file shown in Figure 5, for example, the links are on the left side of the screen. Note the various folders and subfolders. For instance, the folder called *ESL* contains four subfolders: *DistanceEd, MAPrograms, NetProjects,* and *Skills.* The *Skills* subfolder itself contains three subfolders: *Grammar, Listening,* and *Writing.*

Each folder contains links to Web pages of interest to the researcher. An organized system like this is highly preferable to an unorganized compilation of bookmarks, as seen in Figure 6. Bookmark files may be compiled and saved even in a public computer lab because the most popular Web browsers (e.g.,

Figure 5. Favorites File Arranged by Topic

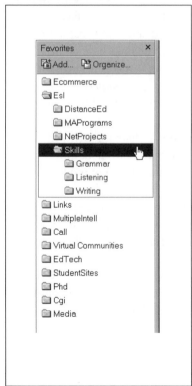

Figure 6. Uncategorized Favorites File

Microsoft Internet Explorer, Netscape Communicator) allow individual users to save bookmarks on a diskette.

The creation of concept maps (introduced earlier in this chapter) and bookmark folders can be successfully combined as follows. Students first create concept maps related to a particular topic, then create a series of folders and subfolders for bookmarks on these topics. The students can then use search tools to find Web pages related to these topics and save links to the pages in the appropriate folders.

Although the Bookmarks and Favorites features are more than adequate tools, other software packages allow more sophisticated categorizing of information. For example, Linkman (1998; see http://www.ourtech.com), a free bookmark management utility, allows users to easily alphabetize bookmark files and export them into editable Web pages to share with others. Shareware for the Macintosh computer called URL Manager Pro (1999; see http://www.url-manager.com) also allows for more complex organization of bookmarks.

On-Line Databases

For people with access to a common gateway interface (CGI) directory, Links 2.0 (1999; see http://www.gossamer-threads.com/scripts/links) is a powerful CGI script for creating and maintaining *Yahoo!*-like databases. CGI scripts are small programs that are placed in a directory on the Web server called *CGI-bin*. They give the Webmaster the ability to go beyond static Web pages to create highly interactive pages, such as on-line databases. The links page of *New Tierra* (http://www.newtierra.com/links), shown in Figure 7, was generated with this script. Each topic on the page (e.g., *Distance Learning, ECommerce, Educational Technology*) is a link to subpages with additional subfolders and ultimately links to resources found to be useful.

Links 2.0 is helpful if you or your class wants to share research with others by making it available on the Internet. With the approval of the database administrator, people who access the page you create can add or modify links to the database. This software is therefore especially effective for allowing groups of students to create and maintain collaborative research sites on the Internet. The administrator can also check through all links for those that lead to expired or dead pages and can immediately and easily delete those links. Installing the script for this software is a bit complicated, but once the script is installed, using the database, adding to it, and modifying it are straightforward. On its Web site, Gossamer Threads (see http://www.gossamer-threads.com), the developer of Links 2.0, lists a help forum where you can find and hire professional assistance in installing the script on your system.

Figure 7. Web Page Generated With CGI Script
(http://www.newtierra.com/links)

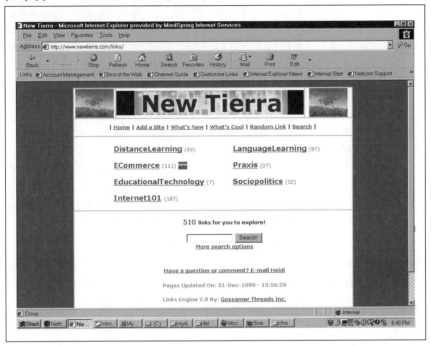

PAIR EXPLORATION AND
DEMONSTRATION OF SEARCH TOOLS

An important goal of using the Internet is to encourage autonomous learning among students. Students will develop effective search strategies not only by following instructions from their teachers but also by exploring the Web on their own and discovering what works and what doesn't. Students also need to learn how to independently investigate, master, and evaluate new search tools as they emerge, because techniques and tools for searching the Web are changing rapidly. By exploring and demonstrating search tools in pairs, students can learn to search the Web, evaluate search tools, and thus become autonomous researchers of effective research tools and processes.

You can organize pair exploration and demonstration of search tools as follows:

1. Have the students form pairs.
2. On the board, an overhead transparency, or a piece of paper, make a list of Web search tools, with at least one search tool listed for each pair of students.

3. Assign each pair, or have each pair choose, a particular search tool to investigate. Give the pairs a specific amount of time (preferably 1–2 hours, either in class or as homework) to explore the tool and its use. The investigation can be structured or unstructured. For example, you might ask teams to (a) consult the help page for the tool to find out the best way to use it, (b) conduct a few sample searches on common topics, or (c) look for special features or offerings (e.g., free e-mail, translation).

4. Have each pair give an oral presentation on the features of the search that includes suggestions for using it effectively and an evaluation of the tool's strengths and weaknesses. If you wish, prepare an empty grid with the names of the search tools as rows and with three columns headed *features, suggestions,* and *strengths and weaknesses.* As a listening and note-taking task, have the class fill in the grid during each pair's presentation. If presentations are given in the computer lab, have the students turn off their monitors so they will pay attention to the presenters.

CRITICAL EVALUATION OF WEB SITES

The World Wide Web contains a vast array of personal, organizational, and commercial information from a variety of sources. A search on *racism* might lead to a paper written by a United Nations agency or a recruitment page for a neo-Nazi group. An article on global warming from the on-line edition of *The New York Times* may link to other articles in *The New York Times'* site or to Web sites developed by business or environmental groups. A page with information on a local university might be created by the university itself, the local chamber of commerce, or a disgruntled student.

Advertisements and content intermingle in a way that often makes it difficult to distinguish between the two. *Yahoo!* (http://www.yahoo.com), once simply the project of two Stanford University undergraduate students, is now owned by one of the largest public companies in the United States and includes on the same page links to news outlets, mortgage lenders, and advertisers. The highly popular *Amazon.com* (http://www.amazon.com), an on-line bookstore, came under criticism when it was learned that its list of recommended books was determined in part by financial contributions from publishers.

The broad array of material on the Web, much of it unlabeled as to source and all of it available with a few clicks of the mouse, makes skills of critical reading and interpretation extremely important. The critical appraisal of Web sites involves the ability to determine and evaluate the source of a Web site; judge the veracity of information on a site; evaluate the point of view behind the content; understand how current the information is; differentiate between commercial, personal, and organizational information; and understand how text, images, graphical display, and linkages all contribute to shaping the presentation of a message.

A number of strategies can assist students in developing skills in critical reading and interpretation. One activity is to have students work in pairs or small groups to evaluate and discuss particular Web sites:

1. Select Web sites that have been created with different purposes in mind, such as a personal Web page, an electronic commerce Web site, a research tool, a discussion board, a nonprofit site for fund-raising, an educational site, and other varied sites. Either create a basic Web page that has links to each of these sites, or simply distribute a list on paper.

2. Give each team a handout or grid with questions to answer (see Figure 8 for an overall question and possible specific questions). You may want to have each team investigate a different site or have two teams investigate the same site to see if they come up with a similar evaluation.

Figure 8. Questions for Web Site Evaluation Activities

Macro question:
- Who created what for whom, when was it created, and with what perceived purpose?

Micro questions:
- Was the Web page created by an individual, an organization, a corporation, or another type of group?
- What is the content of the Web page? Is it a list of links, an article, a brochure, a book, an archive, a company Web page, or something else?
- Who is the target audience of the Web page? How do you know?
- Why do you think the authors created the Web site: for marketing, as an instructional or educational tool, as a storefront, as a communication center, or for some other reason?
- Is the Web page designed to collect users' input for a specific reason? If so, does the site have a privacy statement (a description of how the page creators use the information they gather about you)?
- Is there a date on the Web site? How recent is the information on the site? Can you tell?
- How accurate is the information on the Web site? Do you see any factual errors?
- What is the point of view or perspective behind the information on the page?
- Are there images on the page? If so, what points do they emphasize?
- What kind of "look" does the page have, and how does it affect the message received by visitors to the page?

3. Have the students report on their evaluation. If students are working in pairs, you can put two or three pairs into small groups to share what they have learned. Students can also write up their evaluations or present them orally to the entire class.

Research Projects

On-line research projects of several types can incorporate the tools and techniques discussed in the previous sections. The relationship between these projects and the practice activities described above may vary from project to project. In some cases, you may want to launch students on complex projects and teach them specific research skills and strategies while they are working on the projects. In other cases, you may want to teach the students about tools and techniques first and then introduce them to more complex projects. The point is that particular search strategies are not ends in themselves but tools to help the students carry out more complex projects.

In this section, we focus on two types of research projects: topic-based and task-oriented, which both involve gathering information from the Internet itself rather than, for example, using the Internet principally to share and discuss information that is gathered through other sources. Of course, in practice, good student-centered projects will involve the use of a variety of ways to gather and share information. (See chapter 3 for projects involving student collaboration over the Internet; see chapter 7 for ways to incorporate various kinds of Internet-based projects into a coherent and purposeful curriculum.)

TOPIC-BASED RESEARCH PROJECTS
Topic-based research involves using the Web to gather information on a particular subject. Topic-based projects can be organized in a wide variety of ways, depending in part on how advanced the students are in the language and how comfortable you and your students are with learner-centered work. Issues to consider when assigning topic-based projects include the following:
- *topic selection:* In some cases you may want to select a topic for the entire class. In other cases students may choose from a narrow range of topics or be given free rein in choosing a topic. In the latter case, it is usually still a good idea to have the students report their topic to you so you can evaluate its appropriateness.
- *research questions:* You may draw up specific questions, or students may work individually or in groups to determine research questions.
- *scope of research:* You may recommend a particular list of Web sites to gather information from (or, in some cases, even restrict students to using particular Web sites). In another situation, students may search

for information anywhere on the Web or may search archives of on-line discussion groups. In many cases, on-line research may be combined with research from print sources.

- *presentation:* Findings can be presented in a traditional written report, a report shared over the Internet with other students in the class (e.g., via e-mail, a student-created Web site [see chapter 5]), or an oral presentation.

On-line, topic-based research can be especially effective for investigating current events because up-to-date information may not be readily available from local or school libraries. For example, beginning-level English students may answer a few questions about a current political or military conflict by visiting a few selected Web sites. Advanced-level students may research the conflict in depth by exploring a range of sites they themselves find on the Web (and possibly supplementing the information they find with on-line interviews with people from the countries involved in the conflict).

TASK-ORIENTED RESEARCH PROJECTS

In task-oriented research, students seek information from the Internet to help solve a problem or perform a task. As in topic-based research, these problems or tasks may range from simple to complex.

Tasks may revolve around communication activities designed for the class. In one sample activity, students may plan an evening on the town in a foreign city, such as New York or London. Using the Web, they may find information related to restaurants, movie theaters, or other locations. They might role-play a telephone call to a friend inviting them to attend the activity.

A more challenging task on the same theme involves planning an entire weekend. For example, students may be given a budget of $500 for a weekend in San Francisco and be told that they will arrive at 10:00 a.m. on Friday and depart at 6:00 p.m. on Sunday. They must then use the Web to decide where to stay, how to get from the airport to the hotel, what sites to see, what to buy, and where to eat. They can report on their trip in writing or in an oral presentation to the class (see Deguchi, 1995).

A more complex project involves the preparation of a newscast. After gathering information from the Web about a range of events, students can put together their own news broadcast (L. Rosen, 1995).

Tasks may involve simulations as well. For example, students might track businesses on the Web in order to make investment decisions (see chapter 7), or gather information on environmental issues in order to propose a solution (Vilmi, 1995) or participate in an international debate. With imagination, you will have no trouble working with your students to come up with research tasks and topics designed to match their own interests while simultaneously developing skills in language and informatics.

Conclusion

Neither the English language nor information technology exists as an end in itself. Rather, both are useful to the extent that they empower learners to achieve their broader goals in academic, vocational, civic, and personal affairs. And being able to locate, evaluate, and make use of the vast amount of information that modern society is putting forth—the majority of which is in English—is of great value. By taking an integrative approach to language and informatics, teachers can help students master the English language on-line research skills required for success in today's society.

Chapter 5

Student Publishing

In this chapter, we discuss
how and why to involve students in
publishing their own work on the
World Wide Web.

In 1924, long before the development of the Internet or even of the computer, French educator Freinet founded the Modern School Movement. Freinet's movement was based on two tenets:

1. Students should become active masters of technology rather than passive recipients.
2. Students learn to understand their reality better when they communicate about it with distant partners (Sayers, 1990).

Based on these tenets, students in Freinet's schools engaged in collaborative exchanges with students in other parts of France and the world. Student publishing was a critical part of these exchanges, with students using printing presses, cameras, tape recorders, and other forms of technology to record and publish their work and share it with their communities and their exchange partners. As Freinet (1969) wrote, "Having something to say, writing to be read, to be discussed, to be responded to critically, this is the grand motivation [for literacy] we should be seeking, and which is realized through classroom printing" (cited in Sayers, 1990, p. 32).

Good pedagogy stands the test of time. Freinet's goals and methods are as important today as they were in the last century, perhaps even more so given the prominent role of information and communication technology. Student publishing projects can still achieve the dual purposes of helping students become active masters of technology while sharing authentic texts with real audiences. Today, however, the preferred publishing medium is the World Wide Web. By authoring and publishing multimedia works on the Web, students can develop important new electronic literacy skills while communicating with a global audience.

The first part of this chapter discusses the changing nature of writing in the current era and the consequences of these changes for the English language classroom. In the second part, we outline a project-based approach to on-line student publishing. In the third part, we give examples of students' Web publishing projects. The technical aspects of Web page creation and production are now fairly easy, thanks to a variety of free or readily available software products. (For details on creating Web pages, see Supplement: How to Make Web Pages.)

Hypertext and the Changing Nature of Writing

While speaking at an educational conference, the associate director of the Computer Writing and Research Labs at the University of Texas at Austin was asked if there was any proof that computer-based teaching is superior to traditional teaching in improving students' writing. She replied,

> Can I prove that on-line writing courses improve students' ability to write traditional essays? No, I can't. I also can't prove that driver's ed courses improve students' equestrian ability. . . . What we're doing is preparing students for the kinds of writing they need in the future. (Syverson, cited in Warschauer, 1999, p. 155)

A good deal of evidence backs up Syverson's assumption that the kinds of writing that are required are going through changes. Whether in government (see Lanham, 1993), business (see Faigley, 1997), or academia (see Warschauer, 1999), multimedia authoring is becoming more and more prevalent. Indeed, one prominent composition scholar has suggested that the standard academic essay may gradually go the way of the short story, continuing to serve as an object of study but used infrequently as a means of communication (Faigley, 1997).

The differences between traditional text and multimedia (see Table 1) suggest the following principles for teachers wanting to integrate Web publishing into the language classroom.

1. *See the Web as a medium, not just a vehicle.* Writing effectively for the Web is different from writing on paper. Although it is possible to have students write out traditional essays and post them on the Web, students will gain broader skills if they learn to produce material

TABLE 1. Traditional Classroom Writing Versus Multimedia Authoring

Products of traditional classroom writing . . .	Products of multimedia authoring and publishing . . .
• Are written texts	• May incorporate written text, graphics, images, sounds, and video
• Are organized in a linear fashion	• May be organized in a nonlinear fashion with content broken up into layered pages that are connected by links
• Are self-contained	• Can include links to external multimedia material
• Are usually written for the teacher	• Are written for a public audience on the World Wide Web
• Are usually created individually	• Are often created collaboratively
• Once completed and turned in, are out of the student's hands and unchangeable	• Once published, are accessible to the student for further changes and updating

targeted for the Web medium. Help students think about what forms of communication are most effective on-line, and then help them learn the language and technical skills to use those forms. Students can do this in part by analyzing Web sites produced by others.

2. *Empower students with autonomy.* It may be faster and easier for you to handle the technical aspects of publishing by taking students' work and posting it on the Web. But if students learn to publish on the Web and manage Web sites themselves, they will gain an independence that will empower them outside the classroom. It is usually worth the extra time to maximize the students' opportunities for control.

3. *Integrate skills.* Students do not learn how to author and publish for a new medium like the Web without extensive opportunities to read, listen, and discuss. Web-based publishing projects can thus provide an excellent opportunity to develop a wide range of language skills, especially if collaborative research and discussion are incorporated into the process.

4. *Think "dual immersion"* (L. Opp-Beckman, personal communication, March 1999). Learning to publish on the Web involves not only language skills but also technical skills. These can be learned in tandem. Don't feel that either you or your students have to be Internet experts

before beginning a project. Involve students in the planning of Web projects, and help them learn what they need as they go along. Think of *just-in-time* learning rather than *just-in-case* learning.

5. *Pay attention to the issue of audience.* Just because something is on the Web doesn't automatically mean someone will read it. Try to find ways to arrange feedback from an authentic audience, such as other students in the class, other students or teachers in the school, a partner classroom in another part of the world, or other outside readers.

6. *Emphasize meaningful communication.* Because Web pages are available to the public and not just the teacher, they can have a real impact on how other people think or what they do. Encourage students to write and publish on topics that have significance to them and their communities.

We believe that the principles above can best be put into practice through project-based learning. In the next section, we describe a project-based approach, discuss its application to Web publishing, and give a number of examples of successful projects.

A Project-Based Approach to Web Publishing

PROJECT-BASED LEARNING

Project-based learning involves the organization of a series of learning activities on a particular theme or topic of relevance to the interests and daily lives of students. Student projects in the English language classroom can "require active student involvement, stimulate higher level thinking skills and give students responsibility for their own learning" resulting in "a student community of inquiry involving authentic communication, cooperative learning, collaboration and problem-solving" (Stoller, 1997, p. 2). By making on-line publishing a key or culminating component of a broader project, you can integrate student publishing with the development of other important language and learning skills and experiences. You can also create an environment where students are expected to use the Internet for producing and sharing sophisticated final products rather than only for chatting.

In planning projects, you need to decide whether students will work individually, with a partner, with a small group, with the entire class, or with one or more partner classes. You can address learners' specific needs and interests through individual project work that encourages them to make decisions that relate to their individual experience. Most teachers find that collaborative projects enhance students' opportunities for negotiation and discussion, although it is, of course, possible to incorporate individual tasks into broader projects.

Depending on the context, you, the students, both you and the students, or another person or organization having a stake in the project will choose the theme or topic of the project. Allowing students maximum leeway to select and shape their own topic of inquiry will likely give them a greater stake in the project. You will need to set the time frame for the project and establish appropriate intermediate steps (e.g., project outlines, tasks, and assignments) to provide sufficient scaffolding for students. Once again, students can be involved in developing their own project plans.

Stoller (1997) illustrates a useful sequence for the development of projects in the language classroom (see Figure 1). The sequence might be adjusted slightly for Web-publishing projects. Steps 4, 6, and 8 might be used to prepare students not only for language demands but also for technical demands. (Of course, when done in the target language, the process of discussing and learning technical tasks also incorporates helpful language practice.)

Many educators recommend alternative methods of assessing project-based work. Assessment can be based in part on students' reflective journals (in writing or via audio), on portfolios of students' work (including early drafts), on students' own evaluation of their work or the work of their group, or on the fulfillment of individual or group learning contracts, in which students negotiate the plans and tasks they will complete as part of a project.

SAMPLE WEB-PUBLISHING PROJECTS

The Web-publishing projects described here were organized by English language teachers in the United States, Germany, Japan, India, Russia, Finland, Sweden, Norway, and China. They can be adapted to any country and to various ages or language levels.

Figure 1. Developing a Project in a Language Classroom

1.	Agree on a theme for the project.
2.	Determine the final outcome.
3.	Structure the project.
4.	Prepare students for the language demands of Step 5.
5.	Gather information.
6.	Prepare students for the language demands of Step 7.
7.	Compile and analyze information.
8.	Prepare students for the language demands of Step 9.
9.	Present the final product.
10.	Evaluate the project.

Adapted from Stoller (1997, p. 6).

Virtual Visits

Virtual Visits (see D. J. Rosen, 1999, http://www2.wgbh.org/mbcweis/ltc/alri
/vv.html) is an adult education project that encourages classes to visit places in
their community and document their visits through writing, photographs, and
the creation of a Web site. Participating students select a theme that is
meaningful for the class to explore, conduct research, and create an informative
Web site that can be used by people in the community who are interested in the
same topic. This process of asking questions, finding answers, and sharing results
on the World Wide Web empowers the students. Along the way, students use the
target language to solve real-world problems, reflect on their experiences with
individual writing, and create and publish a joint Web site about the experience.

For example, one class from the East Boston Harborside Community
Center in Massachusetts made a virtual visit to a computer store to learn about
buying a computer (see East Boston Harborside Community Center, n.d.,
http://www2.wgbh.org/mbcweis/esquare/virtualfront.htm). In groups, students
chose a computer system to meet the needs of a scenario presented to them. The
project involved taking pictures at the store, writing as a group, creating a Web
page, and keeping individual journals about the experience that were posted on
the project's Web page.

In another virtual visit, called *Homebuying for Everyone* (Community
Learning Center n.d., http://www2.wgbh.org/mbcweis/ltc/final/vvhome.html),
students in Cambridge, Massachusetts, in the United States, researched how low-
income people can purchase their own homes. First, the students brainstormed
questions they expected people to have about purchasing homes. After doing
Internet research on home buying, they visited a local bank and interviewed
people about getting a loan to purchase a home. Afterward, the group visited a
local organization called the Cambridge Homebuyers Program and interviewed
staff and clients. In the end, the students documented what they had learned on
the Web site created by the class. (For additional home-buying information for
ESL students in the United States, see *Adult ESL Homeownership Education*,
1999, http://www.cal.org/public/fannie.htm.)

Two adult educators have organized a project called A Virtual School Visit
(see Gaer & Rosen, 1999, http://www.otan.dni.us/webfarm/emailproject/school
.htm). Participating in this project are elementary, secondary, and adult
education English language classes from around the world. Students at each
school write about their lives and schools, take pictures of their schools, and post
their work on the Web to share with partner classes. Students from the various
schools then contact each other via e-mail and "virtually visit" each other's
schools on the Web, following up their visits with more e-mail questions and
discussion.

Culture and Community Pages

Optional language classes at the Institut für Anglistik/Amerikanistik in Dresden, Germany, create innovative Web sites in small collaborative groups for the *German Culture Pages in English* (see Ogbue, 1999, http://www.geocities.com /Athens/Forum/8383). One of their projects, called Sächsische Schweiz for Students, is an excellent example of a student-developed Web site. The site contains advice for traveling in Königstein and Rathen in Germany, and in the Czech Republic. For each place, students have included a written essay, a featured photograph, a map, and travel instructions. Students negotiated the content and design of the Web site among themselves, did all of the research, and created the Web pages. A critical component of this project is the requirement that students write journals about the process of doing the project.

Students at Kyoto Sangyo University in Japan have worked on several collaborative projects that have culminated in the creation of Web pages about Japanese history and culture. The *Kyoto Restaurant Project* (Kitagawa, n.d., http:// www.kyoto-su.ac.jp/information/restaurant) presents student reviews of local restaurants; the *Japanese Food Recipe Page* (Kitagawa, Gotou, Saito, Sakamoto, & Sakane, 1997, http://www.kyoto-su.ac.jp/information/recipes) features the students' favorite recipes; and *Famous Personages in Japan* (Robb, n.d., http://www .kyoto-su.ac.jp/information/famous) offers brief biographies of many famous people in fields such as literature, movies, music, politics, and sports.

The *Kyoto Restaurant Project* was the inspiration for the *WOW! Washington on the Web* student project (Meloni, 1999, http://gwis2.circ.gwu.edu/~gwvcusas /WOWHOME.htm), in which students write reviews of restaurants and museums in Washington, DC, in the United States. At the beginning of each semester, the students choose a restaurant and a museum that the class will visit together. After each visit, the students collaborate on a review that serves as a model for subsequent individual reviews. Photographs are always taken during the class outings and included with the reviews on the Web. Students are also encouraged to have their photographs taken when they make their individual visits so that they can be posted along with the reviews.

Travel Diaries

Students in an elective course at the University of California, Santa Barbara, in the United States, called English Through Web Page Creation (see Shetzer, 2000a, http://www.newtierra.com/ucsb) learn how to create and maintain their own Web sites in the context of a 10-week writing project. Students control the content and design of their individual Web sites but must complete specific writing and photography assignments each week. Many students create travel diaries that document their experiences living in the United States, away from their home countries. The project guidelines are open and flexible to encourage student autonomy in topic selection and writing; the students each negotiate a contract as to the work they will perform. Students can store their Web sites on temporary space provided by the university or at free Web server sites on the Internet. The latter is a popular choice among students because they can continue to work on their Web sites without interruption after the course is over.

Environmental Studies Documentary

To study the changes taking place in the local community, students at Miyazaki International College, in Japan, work on the *Environmental Change Documentary* (see Isbell & Reinhardt, 1998, http://www.miyazaki-mic.ac.jp/classes/fall98/aisenv/projects/project1.html), which involves photography and writing. During the course of a semester, students choose one location to photograph each week as a means of observing the changes taking place in the environment. Locations include construction sites, fields, and the Kiyotake River. Each student documents a different environment across time and creates a Web site. The sites, which are designed by individual students, each contain a slide show, written in the JavaScript programming language, that rotates the students' pictures taken across time. Original writing by the students describes the degree of change observed throughout the project.

Endangered Animals

Middle school students in an advanced writing class in New Delhi, India, worked on a collaborative project called Endangered Animals of India (see American Embassy School, 1998, http://cyberfair.gsn.org/falcon/narrative.html). Part of the project involved creating a giant Web site that describes several endangered animals in the country. Students conducted research in the library, on the Internet, on a field trip to the Wildlife Museum of New Delhi, and via interviews with animal specialists at the World Wildlife Fund. After the research, students created Web pages to showcase their findings about endangered animals.

Coast to Coast Project

The Coast to Coast Project (Meloni & Braunstein, 1999, http://gwis2.circ.gwu.edu/~gwvcusas/coasttocoast.htm) brings together intensive English classes at two U.S. universities, the George Washington University and the University of California, Santa Barbara. Students in these classes work together to compare and contrast U.S. culture in each of their settings based on interviews with native speakers of English. The goal of the course is to simultaneously improve students' knowledge of English, U.S. culture, and technology, and the project's Web site serves as a publishing medium and a place for the exchange of information between the two classes.

This 9-week project includes several additional tasks and activities. For example, students prepare a variety of documents and exchange them with the partner class, including biographies and photographs of individual students that are posted on a Web site and writing by individual students that describes their feelings about the city in which they are living. Students also create and exchange culture packages that contain both personal messages for their partner group and artifacts from the local culture. The project culminates in the writing of comparison-contrast essays about the two cities, which are also published on the Web site.

King's Road Project

The King's Road Project (see Vilmi, 1998, http://www.hut.fi/~rvilmi/King) is a collaborative endeavor undertaken by students and teachers in Finland, Norway, Sweden, and Russia. The elaborate project, named after the famous King's Road that runs through each of those countries, aims to bring students and teachers together to discuss issues in their local cultures in order to promote international understanding and cooperation. Students in each locale first work with a traveling theater group from England to create, act out, and write down a student-generated play, which is shared with the other locations via the World Wide Web. Students in the next city down the road read about the experiences of other groups and continue the tradition via creation, performance, and writing on a Web page.

Essentially, the project results in a large, collaborative, creative work published on the Web by students along the King's Road. Students along the road also do research and writing on their locales for presentation to the entire group via the Web. Finally, students from one location on the King's Road travel in person to the next site to give live presentations on their cities.

English Spark

In one of several Web publishing projects, a technical communications class at the Chinese University of Hong Kong worked for 13 weeks to produce the *English Spark Online Magazine* (1996, http://humanum.arts.cuhk.edu.hk/~cmc /engspark; see Figure 2 and Jor, 1995). The students formed teams early in the semester to conduct research on various aspects of technical communication. Throughout the semester, the students attended many workshops on various aspects of news writing and on-line publication. They also learned technical skills related to downloading information from the Web, scanning and uploading graphics, and doing page layout and design. A class editorial board collectively established editorial standards and worked to maintain them. Students worked in their teams and editorial bodies to edit each other's work. The end result was an attractive on-line magazine with original articles on various aspects of technical communication.

Figure 2. *English Spark Online Magazine*
(http://humanum.arts.cuhk.edu.hk/~cmc/engspark)

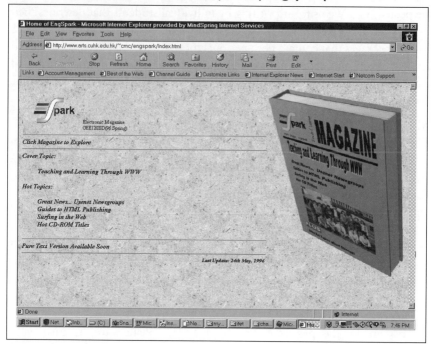

ThinkQuest

ThinkQuest (see http://www.thinkquest.org) is a million-dollar international competition for teenage students around the world. Students form teams in order to plan, design, create, and publish educational Web sites. Teams earn points for their scholarship and creativity and receive extra points if the team members come from different countries. Winning Web sites in 1998 were on a broad range of educational topics, with titles such as *Dolphins: The Oracles of the Sea, The Living Africa,* and *Driving Under the Influence.* ThinkQuest continues annually; details on the contest are available at the project's Web site.

Conclusion

The projects described in this chapter indicate the great variety of ways that Web publishing can be successfully incorporated into the English language classroom. Although the projects differ in many ways, they all integrate a wide range of language skills, teach both language and technology, and tap students' creativity. The result is the development and publication of meaningful works for authentic audiences.

Chapter 6

Distance Education

In this chapter, we introduce
on-line distance education,
examining programs for English
language learners and TESOL
professionals.

I magine that, as a language learner or educator, you can take any course you want at your convenience from your home or office, studying at your own pace. The course is inexpensive and highly individualized to meet your particular needs, yet it allows a great deal of interaction with the instructor and other students.

Now imagine another scenario. The distance education course you've signed up for has far less content than you could find in an average textbook. On-line materials are poorly prepared and hard to access, and there is little opportunity to interact with other students or the instructor, who is not a trained teacher. The course is inexpensive, but because of cost competition, high-quality programs in the community are losing enrollment, and qualified teachers are being laid off.

Which of the above scenarios best characterizes on-line distance education? The truth is probably somewhere in between.

What Is Distance Education?

Until recently, the term *distance education* brought correspondence courses to mind. Profit and nonprofit organizations offered a wide variety of courses for students who were unable to attend classes for one reason or another. Students could stay in their own homes, complete the assignments, and mail them to an address at a distant location. Students could take individual courses for no credit or a series of courses for a certificate, a diploma, or a degree. Students were sometimes, but not always, required to complete a portion of the work at the organization's center. It was possible to receive a university degree without ever having set foot on a college campus.

Although traditional correspondence courses are still available today, the fastest growing segment of the distance education market is based on on-line learning. The principle is the same. Students stay in their homes or offices and complete their assignments, but they communicate via the Internet instead of the postal service. Courses are offered on-line not only by educational organizations such as colleges and universities but also by textbook companies, software companies, enterprising instructors, and other entrepreneurs. In theory, the power of computers and the Internet can allow distance education programs to be more flexible, interactive, and fast-paced, but whether this will prove to be true in practice remains to be seen.

This chapter first considers on-line courses for students who wish to study English—from simple tutorials to full-fledged academic, credit-bearing courses. The second section considers courses designed for current or future teachers that lead to certificates or degrees in TESL/TEFL. Our description of these courses does not indicate an endorsement by us or by TESOL; our intent is to give an overview of currently available on-line courses. We conclude by examining some of the general policy issues related to distance education via the Internet.

On-Line English Language Courses

Opportunities to study English on-line are exploding. The large number of new programs with little track record makes it difficult to choose among them. The following are some of the variables affecting on-line English courses:

- *content:* Some courses focus on particular skills, such as writing, whereas others cover general English. In addition, just as other English classes do, on-line courses vary according to level.
- *pacing:* Some on-line tutorials permit students to join the learning program at any time and let the students control the pacing. Others follow a classroom model more closely, with regularly scheduled synchronous classroom meetings and asynchronous discussions organized by a teacher.
- *the teacher's role:* Some instructors are simply monitors who occasionally drop in on their students in chat rooms whereas other teachers

simultaneously wear the hats of materials creator, technical trouble-shooter, and classroom teacher.

- *instructional materials:* On-line courses often make use of traditional textbooks or materials that are created by the teacher and simply posted on a World Wide Web site. Some on-line courses, on the other hand, are virtual textbooks that contain multimedia drill-and-practice activities packaged with attractive graphics and animations.
- *technology:* Whereas some on-line courses are relatively low-tech, using e-mail, text-based Web pages, or both, others make use of multimedia Web pages, chat rooms, and commercial distance education packages such as WebCT (1999; see http://209.87.17.102/webct), Confer V (1989; see http://www.wmich.edu/docs/3803.html), and Nicenet's *Internet Classroom Assistant* (http://www.nicenet.org).
- *credit:* Some on-line language courses offer credit in degree-granting institutions, others offer certificates, and many others offer neither credit nor a certificate.
- *cost:* On-line language courses range in price from free to expensive.

Students will want to think carefully about all of the above variables in selecting an on-line course.

FINDING ON-LINE ENGLISH COURSES

Lists of on-line courses can be found at *Online ESL Courses* (n.d., http://members.tripod.com/~towerofenglish/onlinecourses.htm). Other Web sites with information on distance learning are listed in Figure 1.

Searching the Web under "English as a second language" and "distance education" or "on-line learning" will also yield a large number of sites. Finally, teachers subscribed to *TESLCA-L* (see Kitao & Kitao, 1999b, http://www.ling.lancs.ac.uk/staff/visitors/kenji/lis-tesl.htm) or *NETEACH-L* (see Moody, n.d., http://www.ilc.cuhk.edu.hk/english/neteach/main.html) will learn about on-line English courses of interest to their students.

CURRENT ON-LINE ENGLISH PROGRAMS

The on-line English courses described here fall into four categories: self-paced free courses, self-paced commercial courses, calendar academic courses, and calendar commercial courses.

Self-Paced Free Courses

Some enterprising English teachers have volunteered their services to help students around the world improve their English by setting up self-paced instruction. Students can join these courses as they wish. *English for Internet* (http://www.study.com) offers free on-line instruction by volunteer teachers to students anywhere in the world. Students may choose real-time or asynchronous

Figure 1. Locating Distance Education Programs

- *Colleges and Universities* (Hoyle, 1999): http://www.hoyle.com/distance/college.html
- *Directory of Online Colleges, Internet Universities, and Training Institutes* (2000): http://www.geteducated.com/dlsites.htm
- *Distance Education Online Symposium (DEOS)* (1999): http://www.ed.psu.edu/acsde/DEOS.html
- *NewPromise.Com: Online Education Directory:* http://www.newpromise.com
- *New Tierra: Distance Learning:* http://www.newtierra.com/links/DistanceLearning
- *Online Courses and Methodology for Learning and Teaching English and French* (Thalman, 2000): http://www.wfi.fr/volterre/onlinecourses.html)
- *SmartPlanet.com:* http://www.smartplanet.com
- *TeleCampus:* http://apsis.telecampus.edu
- *Virtual High School:* http://vhs.concord.org
- *Virtual University:* http://www.vu.org
- *World Lecture Hall:* http://www.utexas.edu/world/lecture
- *Yahoo! Education: Distance Learning:* http://dir.yahoo.com/Education/Distance_Learning
- *Yahoo! Education: Distance Learning: K–12:* http://dir.yahoo.com/Education/Distance_Learning/K_12

classes in preparation for the Test of English as a Foreign Language; English for special purposes; listening, speaking, and pronunciation; grammar and writing; English for Internet; and language and culture.

Online English (Rossetti, 1997, http://www.geocities.com/Athens/Olympus/9260/online.html) is available free to students. After students sign up for a course, they receive lessons by e-mail once a week.

A volunteer teacher for an on-line course writes of his experience as a writing tutor:

> Distance Ed requires a high level of [student] commitment/discipline, possibly more so than what is needed for classrooms in which there's regular face-to-face contact with an instructor and other students. Very few of the students who initially expressed interest actually took advantage of the tutorials. [But] a lot of effective learning can occur with a minimum of technology. I had some very successful tutorials, all of which were accomplished inexpensively via e-mail. (D. Weasenforth, personal communication, April 1999)

Self-Paced Commercial Courses

International House Net Languages (http://www.netlanguages.com) promotes itself as "the world's leading virtual language school." New students in the program first take a placement test and then download materials for home study. Each course includes 120–150 hours of study material. Course units including reading and listening passages, vocabulary and grammar exercises, writing assignments, suggested topics for on-line chats with other students, and tests. Students send their completed written work to a private tutor and can also telephone their tutor to discuss their work. Registered students may also access extracurricular material at the Web site, including an on-line library with videos, readers, grammar books, dictionaries, and a thesaurus. Students are issued a certificate for completing courses.

Aspera PrivaTeacher (see http://www.PrivaTeacher.com) offers a content-based program that functions as an electronic textbook and incorporates teacher-student interaction. The four levels of difficulty each contain various thematic units for students to complete at their own pace. Each unit has reading, listening, grammar, pronunciation, and writing components. Students can check their progress with on-line quizzes. Scores are recorded and compiled for each student and are noted on the students' completion certificates. Students can complete their work on-line or work with the same modules delivered on a CD-ROM. Writing assignments for the thematic course modules in each level are submitted to a writing instructor, who responds with feedback via email. Students also take writing quizzes during the course. Finally, teachers organize on-line chat sessions, which are based on readings from external Web sources.

Englishtown (http://englishtown.com) is an on-line language school that offers a large number of self-paced courses. Students who would like to use *Englishtown*'s resources for self-study without the assistance of a teacher may do so for free, but courses with a teacher are offered on a commercial basis. Students begin with a placement test that is a combination of grammar and listening comprehension. After placing into a level, students can choose General English, Business English, or one of several industry-specific English courses. Courses integrate multiple skills. Testing of students is automated and checked by the computer. For extra practice, students can drop in to prescheduled chat sessions with others in their level during the week. These sessions are organized and monitored by a teacher, who provides feedback to students either privately or in the group. Students can eventually earn a certificate of language study if they complete learning units and meet specific participation, attendance, and performance requirements.

Calendar Academic Courses

Calendar courses are delivered during specific sessions rather than on a drop-in basis. Such courses carry a fee and are offered by academic and commercial institutions.

A number of academic departments offer writing courses on-line. One example is English for Writing Up Research (see *English for Specific Purposes,* 1999, http://www.dundee.ac.uk/languagestudies/esp2.htm#research) at the University of Dundee, in Scotland. This thesis-writing course, for international students studying at the university and living in Dundee, lasts for 6 weeks. Students meet in person with their teacher at the beginning of the course to learn how to use WebCT (1999), a software product, and then take the course on-line throughout the term. This arrangement is convenient, as the students are pursuing degrees in different academic departments and have varying schedules. Each week the class focuses on a topic related to writing a thesis, such as the outline, the introduction, the body/development, the conclusion, the abstract, and the bibliography and acknowledgments. Students are required to view course materials and complete on-line tasks early each week and meet for on-line discussion later in the week (Catterick, 1999). The teacher posts discussion questions for the students before the live chat meetings so they can prepare for substantive discussions in the on-line forum.

Students all over the world can enroll in Advanced English Composition Online for International Students (1999, http://vms.cc.wmich.edu/~kubota /englishonline99.htm) at Western Michigan University, in the United States. The 3-month course focuses on academic expository writing and grammar. Writing assignments include an autobiography; description, comparison and contrast, and argumentation essays; and a research paper. Reading material consists of on-line newspapers, books, and magazines as well as Web pages created by the teacher. The course's centralized Web site includes a course description and weekly schedule that links to on-line resources used in the course. During the course, students use e-mail, word-processing software, and a Web browser as well as the on-line conferencing software Confer V (1989) for synchronous discussion. When students complete a writing assignment, they send it to the instructor, who converts it into a Web page so that the other students can read, review, and discuss it. Students take two tests and a final exam for this noncredit course. Those who complete 65% of the assignments with a grade of C or higher receive a certificate of completion.

Calendar Commercial Courses

A number of commercial institutions also offer calendar courses. For example, *NetLearn Languages* (http://www.nll.co.uk), based in London, England, offers interactive courses for students of English who prefer a group-oriented classroom. Course offerings include general classes, business classes, exam skills classes, one-to-one classes, and programs tailored to corporate clients and other groups. The courses start and end at prescribed dates set by the institution and have a maximum class size of six students. Students are placed in a level from elementary to advanced after taking a placement test that incorporates grammar and vocabulary components. According to E. Baber (program director, personal communication, April 1999), the courses are taught in a communicative fashion and include discussions, debate, peer correction, and peer teaching. Microsoft NetMeeting (1999), software that integrates the exchange of video images, audio, chat, and documents through a shared white board, is used in the program. Students do not purchase regular textbooks for the course, nor do they use any particular on-line textbook. Instead, the instructor gives the students lessons that are cut and pasted into the white board feature of NetMeeting.

On-Line Courses for Teachers of English

Current and future English language teachers might also want to take advantage of the opportunities for professional development made possible by distance education on-line. They may take courses leading to certificates and degrees in TESL/TEFL as well as other courses of interest.

As is true with regard to on-line courses for students, no single clearinghouse of information on on-line TESL/TEFL courses exists. Strategies for finding courses include searching the Web, consulting the resources listed in Figure 1 (see above), and raising questions on *NETEACH-L* and *TESLCA-L.*

TESL/TEFL GRADUATE DEGREE PROGRAMS

The University of Surrey (http://www.surrey.ac.uk), in England, offers an MA in linguistics (TESOL), distance-learning mode, for individuals wanting to teach language. The program is offered completely on-line. There is no residency requirement, and scholarships are sometimes offered to teachers in developing countries. The program is organized in a series of core modules. Students complete the assignments for a module and receive individual feedback via e-mail or audiotape; discussion takes place on an e-mail list. The university also offers a separate MS in English language teaching management that is made up of a series of required and optional modules.

Newport Asia Pacific University (http://www.asiapacificu.edu) offers courses for an MS in TESOL. The 2-year program consists of ten 8-week on-line courses (taken from anywhere) and two 4-day live seminars in Tokyo. Students not pursuing the MS can enroll in individual courses and receive a certificate for each course.

TESL/TEFL CERTIFICATE PROGRAMS

Open Learning International (http://olionline.com), with offices in Spain and England, offers four on-line programs: certificate in TEFL to adults, certificate in TEFL to young learners, diploma in TEFL, and certificate in management of TEFL/TESL centers. The courses consist of 120–260 hours of study and provide flexible learning options. According to information on Open Learning International's Web site, participants can determine the pace of learning, negotiate their own deadlines, and determine whether they will work principally on their own or interact often with fellow students via the Internet.

LEARNING TO TEACH ON-LINE

NetLearn Languages (http://www.nll.co.uk) offers an on-line program leading to a certificate in the on-line teaching of English. This training course gives participants the opportunity to meet synchronously and asynchronously to discuss how to teach on-line with interactive communication tools. Participants first complete a precourse task, which involves research and reflective writing on a variety of topics and activities related to teaching on-line. The results are posted on the course's Web site and discussed by the group. Using Microsoft NetMeeting (1999), participants discuss on-line teaching methodology and materials conducive to teaching in an on-line environment. Through the software, they participate in a variety of seminars, which cover topics such as the use of NetMeeting and other communication tools for synchronous and asynchronous communication, the creation and use of materials, copyright issues, and strategies for teaching on-line. The teacher education program offers opportunities for practice teaching during the course. At first, trainees team-teach a course through NetMeeting, and then they teach on their own. When teaching, student teachers are observed by their classmates and the course instructor. These experiences are then discussed within the group.

A number of universities offer more general distance-learning courses on on-line education. For example, 4-week seminars given over the Internet by the University of Wisconsin—Madison's Distance Education Certificate Program (2000, http://uwex.edu/disted/depd/certpro.html) include Introduction to Online Learning, Group Processes for Online Learning, and Designing for Online Learning.

Finally, there are many opportunities to attend conferences, workshops, and seminars on-line without enrolling in formal courses. The most important of these as related to the field of TESOL are presented in chapter 2.

Conclusion: Issues in Distance Education

The growth of distance learning offers teachers and students many new opportunities but also presents many challenges. The increasing role of commercial companies in distance education poses a threat to traditional academic institutions and may create pressure for mass, low-quality education. There is a concern that a small number of "superstars" will develop on-line course materials and that courses themselves may be taught by untrained assistants. Related to this issue is the question of who controls the electronic materials that teachers develop. If the ownership of the materials passes over to their employers, teachers fear that they might lose control over who uses the materials and how they are used.

The potential dangers of commercialized distance education are catching the attention of educators. In *Distance Learning: Promise or Threat?*, Feenberg (1999, http://www.rohan.sdsu.edu/faculty/feenberg/TELE3.HTM) writes,

> Once the stepchild of the academy, distance learning is finally taken seriously. But not in precisely the way early innovators like myself had hoped. It is not faculty who are in the forefront of the movement to network education. Instead politicians, university administrations and computer and telecommunications companies have decided there is money in it. (n.p.)

Some faculty are beginning to protest threatening trends in distance education. Faculty members at York University in Canada went on strike to defend their ownership of electronic materials they create. Noble (1998, http://communication.ucsd.edu/dl/ddm3.html), writing in *Digital Diploma Mills*, describes a letter signed by several hundred faculty members in the state of Washington, in the United States, in protest to speeches given by Washington's governor praising digital education. The letter reads,

> We feel called upon to respond before quixotic ideas harden into disastrous policies. While costly fantasies of this kind present a mouth-watering bonanza to software manufacturers and other corporate sponsors, what they bode for education is nothing short of disastrous. . . . Education is not reducible to the downloading of information, much less to the passive and solitary activity of staring at a screen. Education is an intersubjective and social process, involving hands-on activity, spontaneity, and the communal experience of sharing in the learning enterprise . . . . (n.p.)

We believe that, as shown by the many examples presented in this book, on-line learning can be an "intersubjective and social process, . . . involving . . . spontaneity, and the communal experience of sharing in the learning enterprise," as the faculty in Washington demand. The technology available offers exciting possibilities for enhancing interaction at a distance. But such results are not ensured. Teachers need to actively participate in determining the direction of distance education so that on-line courses and programs are developed with teachers' and students' interests in mind. Teachers should join together to demand that distance education programs maintain standards of staffing, program quality, and assessment. And educators should certainly work to keep ownership and creative control of their own products and materials.

Most important, as education extends from the classroom to the computer screen, we should never lose sight of the human factor in learning. Language learning, more than almost any other discipline, is a social endeavor.

Chapter 7

Putting It All Together

In this chapter, we examine the basic principles and some models for incorporating the Internet into English language courses.

A s discussed throughout this book, the Internet is dramatically altering how people read, write, and communicate. The Internet is so vast and complex that learning how to incorporate it effectively into the language classroom can be quite challenging. The challenge seems even more daunting because of how quickly the Internet continues to change. For all these reasons, learning how to use the Internet for teaching has been compared to trying to get a drink of water from a gushing fire hydrant!

Nevertheless, we believe that keeping some basic principles in mind makes the process simpler and clearer. These principles relate to pedagogy rather than to technology, and in that sense they should remain useful guides even as particular tools change. We divide these principles into learning goals, teaching guidelines, and planning tips.

Learning Goals

According to a Chinese proverb, it doesn't matter how fast you travel if you're going in the wrong direction. Before thinking about how to plan a lesson or a semester, first consider the overall objectives. The various goals and objectives of

English language courses vary from course to course and among individual students. In this section, we briefly discuss the particular goals that we think should accompany the use of the Internet and complement other linguistic or educational goals.

ACTIVE AND CREATIVE MASTERY

Even though information technologies are becoming ubiquitous, too many people use them in only a passive fashion. As noted in chapter 5, we as teachers are shortchanging our students if we do not help them achieve active and creative mastery of new technologies, not only for receiving information and knowledge but also for collaboratively producing them. This mastery will enhance students' opportunity to actively shape the multimedia future.

AUTONOMOUS LEARNING

Because information technologies are changing so quickly, mastery is not a onetime goal but an ongoing, lifelong process. Students must not only learn but also "learn to learn," that is, develop the autonomous learning strategies needed to adapt to new technologies and new situations. This ability will aid students in achieving the types of benefits that will long outlast one particular course.

COLLABORATIVE LEARNING

Collaborative learning is often seen as a means in the English language classroom. We believe that now it is not an optional means but an extremely important means and end. In the age of the Internet, the ability to cooperate and collaborate with other partners in the same institution or across the world is essential to success, and students cannot really learn to use the Internet well unless they learn collaborative communication and teamwork skills.

CROSS-CULTURAL LEARNING

Just as the Internet enhances the importance of collaborative learning, it also magnifies the importance of cross-cultural learning. Success in today's Internet-connected global society—whether in the business world, academia, or civic affairs—depends in large measure on the ability to communicate effectively with people from different cultures and interpret information from varied cultural contexts. This goal, too, should be consciously integrated into the Internet-enhanced classroom.

CRITICAL LEARNING

Finally, the vast amount of information available on the Internet means that critical learning and literacy skills are more important than ever before. More than ever, reading now means reading between the lines. We as teachers should help learners think critically at the microlevel, for example, by analyzing the perspectives and biases of individual World Wide Web sites. We should also help learners think critically at the macrolevel by considering how new information technologies are helping reshape social, political, and economic contexts in a broader sense.

Teaching Guidelines

The five learning goals listed above—active and creative mastery, autonomous learning, collaborative learning, cross-cultural learning, and critical learning—are important elements to consider in any English language classroom in today's society. They take on even greater meaning and importance in relation to the goals of incorporating the Internet into teaching. The teaching guidelines in this section will help you organize your classes to achieve the above goals as well as specific learning objectives in areas of second language development.

DUAL IMMERSION
Traditional approaches to computer-assisted language learning (CALL) view technology as a tool for teaching English. In our view, this perspective is too limited in a world where technology has drastically altered how language may be taught and how language is used daily around the world. To learn effective communication skills, students thus must learn the English language and the technology together.

L. Opp-Beckman (personal communication, March 1999) has suggested a framework for accomplishing this, which she calls *dual immersion*. In dual immersion, students are immersed in learning language skills and technology skills simultaneously, with the teacher providing the necessary structure and support along the way. This framework closely matches what we have found to work in our own courses and in those we have researched (see, e.g., Warschauer, 1999). It is also consistent with what we have called an *electronic literacy approach* (Shetzer & Warschauer, 2000), which emphasizes the importance of developing new technology-enhanced literacy and communication skills in the English language classroom.

INTEGRATION
Dual immersion is best achieved if computers are well integrated into the curriculum. As Warschauer (1996b) notes, CALL has gone through three stages: behavioristic (beginning in the 1970s), communicative (beginning in the 1980s), and integrative (beginning in the 1990s). Behavioristic CALL emphasized drill-and-practice software for the learning of discrete skills. Communicative CALL focused on communicative activities using the computer but often still in an ad hoc or disconnected fashion, leading many to conclude, as Kenning and Kenning (1990) stated, that CALL "finds itself making a greater contribution to marginal rather than to central elements" (p. 90) of language learning. This led to an interest in integrative CALL, in which the computer is used

naturally and regularly together with other tools and media "serving the creation of an enriched workplace for accessing resources and using language constructively" (Barson & Debski, 1996, p. 52). Indeed, research in a variety of classroom and organizational settings has provided evidence that the introduction of computers has the most impact when the computers are an integral component of a new way of learning and working instead of being used in an isolated fashion (see, e.g., Sandholtz, Ringstaff, & Dwyer, 1997; Zuboff, 1988). In CALL, therefore, try to think of how Internet-based activities can become part of and support the overall class curriculum rather than how to use them in isolation.

PROJECT-BASED LEARNING

Integrated teaching demands new ways of organizing the classroom. Probably the most important of these is the incorporation of project-based learning (see chapters 3, 4, and 5 and the examples in this chapter). When students work together on substantive projects, they gain experience in developing their own learning goals and using the Internet as a resource to fulfill these goals. They can also solve problems and carry out tasks that are similar to what they will later have to do outside the classroom. Project work can also help ensure that Internet activity moves beyond simple chatting or Web surfing. Rather, simpler tasks (e.g., chatting with a keypal or browsing the Web) lead to more complex products, such as an oral presentation or an on-line publication. Project work is an excellent way to help achieve all of the goals mentioned above.

STUDENT-CENTERED LEARNING

Project work goes hand-in-hand with another suggested approach, student-centered learning. Student-centered learning implies that the course curriculum in general, and student projects in particular, will be shaped according to students' own needs and interests. This ability to adapt the curriculum matches the requirements of the new information economy and society, in which people must be able to find and create different types of knowledge as they need them rather than apply facts that they have learned in school (Reich, 1991).

Student-centered learning does not imply that the teacher is absent or passive but rather assumes that the role of the teacher shifts from the proverbial "sage on the stage" to that of a "guide on the side" (Tella, 1996, p. 6), helping students organize their projects and giving language-specific instruction as needed during project activities. Several research studies have indicated that when teachers are able to make such a shift, computer- and Internet-enhanced learning has more positive results (e.g., Sandholtz, Ringstaff, & Dwyer, 1997; Warschauer, 1999).

LEARNING WITH A PURPOSE

The Internet allows even children to find and access important information and communicate to a real audience. The Internet is thus well suited for sustaining projects with a meaningful purpose. Students can work in long-distance teams to tackle an environmental issue (Vilmi, 1995) or help build a Web site for a local nonprofit agency (Warschauer, 1999). They might explore common ground on an international conflict (Cummins & Sayers, 1995) or write a policy statement for a global treaty (Mak & Crookall, 1995). There are many choices for student projects. Finding one connected to a real-world purpose will ensure that students learn not only how to "surf the Web" but also how to "make waves" (Shneiderman, 1997, p. vii).

Planning Tips

Putting these guidelines into effect can be a complex process, especially in light of the additional complexities of using computer laboratories and accessing the Internet (see Figure 1). Here are some planning tips:

- *time:* Be aware that on-line projects take a lot of time to implement. It is better to do a few tasks or projects and do them well rather than to take on too much the first time. Start with something clear and relatively straightforward, and add new dimensions in future semesters if you wish. For example, *WOW! Washington on the Web* (Meloni, 1999, http://gwis2.circ.gwu.edu/~gwvcusas/WOWHOME.htm; see chapter 5) began with reviews of restaurants; students themselves later asked to add reviews of other institutions, such as museums and theaters.

- *computer and Internet access:* If possible, make sure ahead of time that students have access to school computers outside class so they can practice on their own. If you have a choice of either hardware or software, choose the most user-friendly types. (See Figure 2 for tips on doing projects when access to computers and the Internet is limited.) Also help students get individual e-mail accounts, either through the school or through a free Web-based e-mail service such as *Yahoo! Mail* (http://mail.yahoo.com) or *Hotmail* (http://www.hotmail.com). Many projects, such as the high school e-mail exchange project described below, can be done entirely by e-mail.

- *communications:* Set up e-mail lists for small groups or the whole class to facilitate interaction either through your institution or through a free on-line service, such as *eGroups.com* (http://www.egroups.com). For example, in the US-SiberLink project (Braunstein, Meloni, & Zolotareva, 1999, http://www.gwu.edu/~washweb/us-siberlink.htm; see chapter 3),

Figure 1. Potholes on the Information Superhighway

1. *slow downloads:* When an entire class uses a laboratory at the same time to visit a handful of sites, the students might experience the "World Wide Wait" rather than the World Wide Web. To avoid this problem,

   • Have students work in groups to minimize the number of Internet connections used.

   • Even better, visit the sites from each computer right before the lesson begins so the sites will be *cached* (i.e., saved) on the computer's browser.

   • Better still, download the entire site onto the computer's hard drive using software such as Teleport Pro (1997; see http://www.tenmax.com /teleport/pro) or WebWhacker (1999; see http://www.bluesquirrel.com /products/whacker/whacker.html).

2. *dead links:* Internet sites change their addresses over time, and Web servers crash, making sites temporarily or permanently unreachable. To minimize this problem,

   • Use larger, well-established sites.

   • Check sites regularly to see that they are still functioning.

   • Most important, orient your students to the fact that Web addresses change and that they may need to conduct their own searches to find updated or alternate resources.

3. *lost in cyberspace:* Using the Web can be a very disorienting experience for students of English, especially those who are at lower English levels or who have minimal experience with computers.

   • Create a friendly home page for your course to give students a secure place from which to begin their Web browsing.

   • Take the time and effort to see that the Web browsers in the laboratory are properly configured (e.g., with the appropriate home page, language, and outgoing e-mail address).

   • Later, if you wish, teach students how to configure the browsers themselves. Also teach students how to bookmark or e-mail themselves their favorite sites so they can visit them later.

students formed small "netgroups" to collaborate by e-mail on their projects.

  • *hands-on training:* The first time you provide hands-on training, try to find one or two assistants to help you, and prepare a clear handout for your students. See *How to Create a Basic Web Page With Netscape Composer* (Shetzer, 1999b, http://www.newtierra.com/composer) and *How to Use WS_FTP in the Storke Lab* (Shetzer, 2000b, http://www

Figure 2. High Tech in a Low-Tech Environment

Are you working in a school with limited access to the Internet, few computers, or out-of-date equipment? Here are some tips especially for your situation:

1. *Focus on e-mail.* Many effective Internet projects can be done with simple text-based e-mail and don't require multimedia.

2. *Combine off-line and on-line work.* Most of the work on successful Internet projects—for example, writing or reading e-mail messages—is done off-line. Students working on a Web publishing project can also do much of their research, writing, and Web page creation off-line, and Web pages can even be stored and viewed on a local computer rather than on the Internet.

3. *Have students work in groups.* Students often benefit from sharing a computer. Even in a one-computer classroom, one group can work at the computer while other groups work on other tasks. For further suggestions, see the following resources:

   - *Ideas for the One Computer Classroom* (Peebles, 1996, http://danenet.wicip.org/mmsd-it/tlc/1comprm.html)
   - *The One Computer Classroom* (Lim, 1998, http://www.remc11.k12.mi.us/bcisd/classres/onecomp.htm)
   - *Strategies and Applications for the One Computer Classroom* (Burkhart, 1999, http://www.lburkhart.com/elem/strat.htm)
   - *Surviving in the One-Computer Classroom* (1999, http://www.techtrain.org/curriculum/1computr.htm)
   - *Using the Internet in the One Computer Classroom* (1997, http://millpark.ddouglas.k12.or.us/onecomp.html)

4. *Make use of computers outside school.* Many international exchange projects have relied on a teacher's home computer to send a weekly report by e-mail. Other possibilities include a computer and Internet connection at a local library, community center, business, or university. You can also make use of students' home computers, but try to do so in a way that includes the students who don't have home computers. For example, one student with a computer and Internet access can find or download information for the entire class.

5. *Learn to make do with an older computer:* NewDeal Inc. (http://www .newdealinc.com) provides low-cost e-mail and Web-browsing software with a full graphical interface that runs on almost any personal computer, including computers with Intel 286, 386, and 486 processors.

.newtierra.com/ucsb/ftp.html) for handouts created for the class English Through Web Page Creation, described in chapter 5. And, if possible, train a couple of students ahead of time to see what problems might arise when you train a whole class (Robb & Tillyer, 1994, as cited in Warschauer, 1995a).

- *partners:* Multiclass projects are especially complex. When choosing partner classes, be aware of differences in schedule, level, or goals. Differences can be managed as long as they are taken into consideration. Collaboration on several such projects (see, e.g., Corio & Meloni, 1995; Meloni & Braunstein, 1999, http://gwis2.circ.gwu.edu/~gwvcusas/coasttocoast.htm, described in chapter 5) was possible in part because the teachers involved were able to find partners whose teaching schedules matched their own.

- *team teaching:* A multiclass project involves close coordination with one or more teachers. Choose a partner who is reliable and, if possible, who has a similar teaching approach. Discuss your goals ahead of time. If several teachers are involved, set up an e-mail list just for the teachers. For example, d'Eça (n.d., http://www.malhatlantica.pt/teresadeca/spiritofxmas.htm) and her partner teacher discussed in detail the goals and activities of the cultural exchange they organized for their classes (discussed below); see the site for copies of their planning messages.

- *student interaction:* Help students in long-distance projects create a hospitable atmosphere before beginning intense project work. Encourage students to introduce themselves and exchange personal information. Have them share artifacts such as pictures, artwork, or school memorabilia (Sayers, 1993) either on-line (see, e.g., the US-SiberLink project, described in chapter 3) or by sending cultural packages in the mail (see, e.g., the high school e-mail exchange project described below).

- *monitoring:* Establish clear guidelines and timetables for on-line projects. If appropriate, involve students in developing the guidelines, but in all cases make sure to communicate them clearly to all participants. See *Culture Web Site Project* (R. S. Davis, 1998a, http://www.esl-lab.com/courses) for a clear list of assignments and a time line for a semester-long, project-based course.

- *assessment:* Explain clearly to students how they will be assessed, and let them know whether you will be monitoring their on-line interaction. Consider evaluating students by means of electronic portfolios, which contain samples of students' computer-based work (see, e.g., A Middle School Web Publishing Project, below.)

- *a shared experience:* Allow students to share their work with other teachers, students, and family or community members through computer or Internet fairs at your school. Also share the experience yourself by writing about it for an on-line discussion list or journal (see chapter 2; see also Robb's 1995/1996 article, which documents an Internet-based project).

Sample Web Projects

The projects described in this section illustrate the ways that teachers are using the Internet in a variety of contexts. The examples include five from K–12 schools and five from universities.

PRIMARY SCHOOL WEBFOLIOS

Rachel Arenstein teaches English at Arazim in Maalot, Israel. Students in her school go to a networked 20-station computer laboratory once a week, and Arenstein decided to use the time to have the students create portfolios on the World Wide Web called *Webfolios* (Arenstein, personal communication, July 1999; n.d., http://www.maltar.org.il/k12/arazim/eng/portfols.htm). In the laboratory, Arenstein worked with fifth- and sixth-grade students who had been studying English since the third grade. The students wrote and designed their Web pages in English themselves using Netscape Composer (a component of Netscape Communicator, 1999). Instructions on how to design the Web pages were given in Hebrew, but the software itself is in English, so using it reinforced the students' language skills. All the students' writing was in English.

Topics and tasks for the portfolios corresponded to the specific elements of a portfolio recommended by the national English Inspectorate of Israel. For example, fifth graders are expected to copy correctly, so the students were asked to copy a jazz chant from their course book. Students are expected to be able to express their feelings in English, so they created a table of their likes, hates, and wants. For a piece of factual writing, students were asked to describe the weather.

Students pursued a variety of strategies in creating the elements of their Webfolios. Some wrote directly on the screen, and others prepared their writing at home. Students also had free rein to choose the backgrounds and fonts for their sites from among those that the teacher had preselected and downloaded onto a graphics page.

Arenstein feels that the project has tapped students' multiple intelligences well. Students can use their artistic skills to design the pages, their writing skills to create the texts, and their interpersonal skills to plan the pages with their classmates. They are highly motivated, and they are learning English and computer skills simultaneously. A downside to the project is that it takes a good deal of time for the children to master the computer skills and carry out the tasks. Arenstein plans on continuing the Webfolio project, and she hopes that the children develop more creative sites after they complete some of the preliminary projects.

A PRIMARY SCHOOL E-MAIL CULTURAL EXCHANGE

Teresa Almeida d'Eça teaches sixth-grade English at Escola de Santo António in Parede, Portugal. D'Eça began a voluntary, after-school e-mail exchange between a small group of her students and some U.S. students (personal communication, July 1999). The after-school project was so successful that she launched a whole-class cultural exchange project via e-mail the following semester as part of her regular curriculum. Full details of the project, including numerous examples of e-mail messages from teachers and students, can be found at *The Spirit of Christmas* (d'Eça, n.d., http://www.malhatlantica.pt/teresadeca/spiritofxmas.htm).

D'Eça located Glenn Rutland, a fifth-grade teacher in Florida, in the United States, who was interested in carrying out a student exchange. The two teachers corresponded by e-mail in September to plan for the e-mail exchange, carefully coordinating the objectives (see Figure 3), activities, and logistics. They chose a number of topics for the exchange, including Christmas decorations, shopping, and the meaning of Christmas. The project itself began in October and lasted until early January.

Students in each class were assigned to groups of five; students of different language levels were intentionally mixed. Students then corresponded group to group, first writing basic messages introducing themselves and then addressing the specific Christmas-related topics. D'Eça taught her students vocabulary that would be helpful in the letters. The students then worked on their messages during class in groups, with d'Eça assisting as needed. The Portuguese students were only in their second year of English and needed a lot of help. As d'Eça put it, "I always had 5–6 students around my desk, so I used to say that I looked like a mother chicken with all the little chicks around her" (personal communication, July 1999).

The class had no access to computers during the school day but could use three or four school computers after school. Volunteers from each group took

Figure 3. Objectives of the Spirit of Christmas Cultural Exchange

1. To establish a social and cultural contact between students from different and distant communities;
2. To share traditions/customs and experiences that may contribute to a better knowledge and understanding of one another;
3. To create and promote research habits;
4. To improve the knowledge of English;
5. To stimulate an interest for reading and writing;
6. To introduce new technologies into the learning process;
7. To make students both producers and publishers of their work;
8. To increase the number of readers of the students' work through the Web.

Source: T. A. d'Eça (personal communication, July 1999).

turns staying after class once a week to type the letters on a computer, with d'Eça providing additional assistance as needed. She then sent the e-mail from her home computer because there was no e-mail access at school.

A highlight of the exchange was when John Glenn became the oldest man ever in space. The Florida students witnessed the space shuttle takeoff during a field trip to the Kennedy Space Center and excitedly shared the news with the Portuguese students, who had watched the event on television.

D'Eça noted a great increase in her students' enthusiasm for English as a result of the project. Their writing skills also improved a good deal because of the extensive practice. And by the end of the semester, the students had made good friends and had even tried recipes sent by their keypals.

At the end of the semester, d'Eça assembled the students' messages into a book, which she placed in the library for others to see. She also put up notices on bulletin boards to let other teachers and students in the school know about the project and book. In spite of the extra work that such projects take, d'Eça is strongly committed to continuing them in the future. She plans on doing one e-mail exchange project each year, tied to the particular curriculum of the students in that year's course.

A MIDDLE SCHOOL WEB PUBLISHING PROJECT

Markus Kneirum and Alexander Mokry teach English and social sciences at Georg-August-Zinn Comprehensive School in Kassel-Oberzwehren, Germany. They developed a Web publishing project for a seventh-grade English class based on the book *K's First Case* (Alexander, 1975), a detective story about a rich man killed by his housekeeper.

According to Kneirum (personal communication, March 1999), most German students' writing experience is restricted to fill-in-the-gap exercises and guided compositions. He and Mokry thus wanted to give their students the opportunity to develop their skill in writing for more natural and communicative purposes. At the same time, they did not want their students to become overwhelmed, so they began the project with exercises and tasks the students were familiar with, moved to guided but independent tasks, and ended by having the students working on their own with minimal teacher control.

Students had three writing assignments for the project. First, they wrote a short summary of the book, making use of a teacher-prepared worksheet with questions and useful expressions. The second writing activity was more open and collaborative, with students working in groups to develop their own ideas on a topic that built on the book's story. For example, some wrote newspaper articles and interviews about the characters, some wrote dialogues between characters, and others wrote TV news reports based on the book's events.

Students spent much time editing, revising, and rewriting their pieces. They were told from the beginning that their writing would be published on the Web, and, according to Kneirum, this knowledge greatly increased their motivation to write well. The writing activities were complemented by other activities designed to foster additional skills. Students were given the option of recording audio or video versions of their written texts, and their work on developing these entailed a good deal of pronunciation practice. Students were also allowed to make their own Web sites and thus gained design and authoring experience. Finally, they wrote personal home pages that were included in the site.

The entire project was completed in a room with one computer for every three students. Although students sometimes had to wait their turn, this encouraged them to work collaboratively and help each other with their writing and Web design.

On the final day of the project, the children visited each other's Web sites and turned in their portfolios. Their grades for the project were based on the quality of their written product (correctness, creativity, and effort), their mark on a vocabulary test (based on vocabulary from the book and on other expressions the students had come across in reading and writing their essays), and an evaluation of their portfolio, which contained all versions of their texts.

According to Kneirum, the project was quite challenging for the students because it imposed new expectations on them. Instead of providing a teacher-centered classroom, the instructors demanded independence. Instead of handing out worksheets, the instructors expected creativity. And instead of working alone, as was usually the case, the students were expected to work in groups. But the fact that the students were working on their own projects to be published on their own home page, which would be subject to public scrutiny, brought out a great deal of motivation, commitment, and creativity, and the students completed the project with great success.

A JUNIOR HIGH VIRTUAL CLASSROOM

Jack Tseng teaches junior high at Ming-Dao School in Taichung, Taiwan. Tseng is obliged to follow a fairly traditional grammar-based curriculum in his course in order to meet the requirements of standardized examinations, and he has no computers in his classroom to use with his students (personal communication, July 1999). But Tseng has created a bilingual virtual classroom on the World Wide Web called *Jack's English Classroom* (http://NetCity1.web.hinet.net /UserData/tseng913), which his students use outside regular class time. Tseng maintains the Web site at a free Chinese language on-line Web-hosting service called *HiNetCity* (http://netcity.web.hinet.net).

The majority of Jack's students use Internet connections at home to access the virtual classroom. The highly interactive site includes an announcement space, a message board, a forum, and a chat room where Tseng and the students meet at designated times. The students sometimes post their homework assignments on the forum and discuss them on-line. On occasion, the class discusses the on-line activities during the regular class period. The virtual classroom has a place for students' Web pages and a link to a Taiwanese site called *Hello* (http://www.hello.com.tw), where students can get free e-mail addresses. Tseng looks forward to the opportunity to use computers more with his students in school. In the meantime, he is glad that many of them are able to practice their English after school in a virtual environment.

A HIGH SCHOOL E-MAIL EXCHANGE PROJECT

Roseanne Greenfield teaches English at Buddhist Sin Tak College, a secondary school in Hong Kong. She has developed a collaborative, task-based e-mail exchange project that is suitable for secondary school English language classes following the syllabus of the standard National Curriculum used in Hong Kong (personal communication, March 1999).

Greenfield's students worked with a class of native English speakers from Mt. Ayr Community in Ringgold County, Iowa, in the United States. The exchange involved three elements: project-based learning, cooperative learning, and process writing, none of which, according to Greenfield, is regularly practiced in Hong Kong. Before the exchange began, Greenfield taught her students to use these elements with their regular textbooks and course materials. For example, when the Hong Kong syllabus called for lessons on discrete grammar skills, such as the use of negative statements or conjunctions, Greenfield had her students practice the same grammar points in meaningful collaborative writing assignments. Students became comfortable with the kinds of project-based learning approaches they would use with their U.S. partners.

In the e-mail exchange, Greenfield's students worked with their international partners on essays in two genres of academic writing, descriptive essays and imaginative essays, which are mandated in the Hong Kong curriculum. Together, the students then edited and produced an anthology of student writing.

As a first step, students exchanged personal letters, which served as an icebreaker for the project. Students then worked in teams at their own site to write descriptive essays about their community setting, focusing on issues such as historical landmarks, tourist sites, architecture, landforms, restaurants, and schools. The students removed some words from the essays to turn them into cloze exercises and sent the essays to their international partners, who tried to fill in the blanks. At about the same time, students exchanged by postal service cultural packets containing such items as photographs of students and their families, menus from local restaurants, coins, stamps, pictures of state birds and flowers, and class videotapes and brochures about school and community events.

In the next stage, students worked in small groups at each home school to propose topics for the imaginative essays. They then negotiated by e-mail to narrow down the topics, finally selecting the theme of entertainment. Within this theme, students could choose a specific topic of their own interest. One student wrote about life as a member of the Shanghai Acrobatics Team. Other essays focused on the imagined life of a country-western singer or a TV news presenter.

Then, using a grading rubric developed by both teachers, students employed peer-editing techniques, first in their home classes and then with their international partners via the Internet. After receiving comments from their peers in both locations, they discussed how the essays could best be published as a student anthology. Via Internet discussion, classes on both sides made editorial decisions about the layout and content of the publication.

According to Greenfield, the project had many benefits, including giving the students a chance to develop their writing skills for a real audience while developing the skills of long-distance negotiation, organization, editing, revision, and editorial production. The project helped students see English as a valuable tool for international communication rather than only as a subject required for the national examination.

AN INTERNET RESEARCH PROJECT IN AN INTENSIVE ENGLISH PROGRAM

Adele Hansen, who teaches business English at the Minnesota English Center of the University of Minnesota, in the United States, structures her course around a major Internet research activity called the Investment Project (personal communication, July 1999). In the project, students use the Internet to research companies they might want to invest in. They then work in teams to follow the stocks and compile an investment portfolio. Finally, they create a Web site based on their research, which forms part of a larger oral presentation they make to their class.

Before the project begins, Hansen introduces basic vocabulary and concepts related to stocks and investing. Students then form groups in the classroom to tentatively plan their investment strategies. They later meet in the computer laboratory, where they use Internet search engines to locate information about the companies they have selected. They also use the Internet to track stock prices.

Hansen then introduces Web site design by asking students to map a particular Web site that is already on the Internet. Students look at one of several assigned sites and draw lines from the main page to each document linked to that page. The class discusses the nonlinear structure of the Web sites and analyzes the uniform elements that appear across sites.

Students then meet in groups to plan the Web site they will produce. Hansen gives each group a list of required elements for the site. For example, each group member must contribute two to three paragraphs of content, each page should contain links to related information, and the site needs to be interesting. Students are also taught how to examine the source code of existing sites in order to learn more about Web site design. Although each student learns all aspects of authoring, in their teams they choose one principal role as a writer, navigator, or designer.

Most of the Web site design is done outside class. Hansen provides some additional Internet resources to help the groups get started, such as *Web66: A K12 World Wide Web Project* (http://web66.coled.umn.edu) or WebFX (1999; see http://www.newbreedsoftware.com/webfx). The project culminates in oral reports on the project, including presentations of the Web sites.

A UNIVERSITY-LEVEL CONTENT-BASED COURSE

Randall Davis taught a content-based language course called Crossing Borders via the Internet in the Department of Intercultural Studies at Nagoya University in Japan (personal communication, July 1999). In the course, the students learned English as they studied (and practiced) intercultural communication. The course was based on a well-structured, 19-lesson syllabus that gave students the opportunity to simultaneously develop their hands-on technical skills, their knowledge about intercultural communication via the Internet, and their language skills.

Early assignments in the course included on-line readings (e.g., *What's the Internet?*, R. S. Davis, 1998b, http://www.esl-lab.com/courses/start.html) and links to enjoyable, interactive Web sites (e.g., *Totally Free Stuff*, http://www .totallyfreestuff.com). Step-by-step, the students then learned to search the Internet, send e-mail messages, join and participate in e-mail discussion lists, and construct a Web page. During the last 5 weeks, the students carried out a culture research project (see R. S. Davis, 1998a, http://www.esl-lab.com/courses/project .html) in which they use a variety of Internet sources to gather information about a holiday in another country. The students' marks in the course were based on their research paper, home page project, attendance and participation, home-work, and exams. Tests for the course were also delivered through an on-line format on a password-protected site; students were given the password on the day of the test.

A UNIVERSITY ON-LINE WRITING COURSE

John Steele's on-line writing class at the University of Puerto Rico, Aguadilla, is set up to maximize students' opportunities to communicate in writing with the instructor and with each other while teaching them to access resources from the World Wide Web (personal communication, July 1999). The course textbook, developed by Steele, is posted on his home page. All students are required to get an e-mail address and to post assignments to him via e-mail. In addition, Steele has set up an electronic classroom using Nicenet's *Internet Classroom Assistant* (http://www.nicenet.org). Students go to this site to find assignments and post their answers to questions. Students must read and comment on their classmates' answers to questions and participate in a class discussion list.

In addition to the students who come to class sessions and also participate on-line, about 10 students take the course entirely on-line. This option provides another means of teaching writing to students who, for reasons of schedule or disability, are unable to attend class sessions.

A UNIVERSITY-LEVEL PROBLEM-BASED LEARNING COURSE

Susan McGregor, who teaches EFL at Université Catholique de Lille in France, has established a course to help students develop their Internet and English skills while solving a practical problem related to their own life goals (personal communication, March 1999). Students in McGregor's Foreign Internship Network Development EFL course use modern communication tools to search for international internship opportunities. The language course focuses on planning projects; preparing curriculum vitae (CVs); developing written communication skills for business letters and e-mail, and oral communication skills for telephone interviewing and follow-up; networking; using the Internet as a resource; and developing cross-cultural understanding.

Students begin the course by doing Internet research on foreign internship opportunities in their own field (e.g., engineering). Having a specific goal in mind allows them to quickly hone their Internet research skills. They use Internet search engines, on-line employment centers, classified ads in on-line newspapers, and company Web sites for their search. As they begin to identify potential employers, students prepare CVs and cover letters. The replies they receive from employers, together with other Internet resources, form a corpus of authentic material that serves as a platform for study and analysis, helping students improve their writing of CVs, business letters, and e-mail messages.

Because students are engaged in authentic and, to them, important communication as part of the course, they are highly motivated to identify weaknesses in their communication skills and seek assistance. They learn to address these weaknesses with the help of the teacher and through independent on-line research. According to McGregor, the course helps students develop language and technical skills as they work on a task important to their own future. It has been most successful with third- and fourth-year students, who have the requisite language skills and other background knowledge to write a good CV and pursue an internship.

A UNIVERSITY ENVIRONMENTAL PROJECT

Ruth Vilmi of Helsinki University, in Finland (teaching an EFL course), George Jor of the Chinese University of Hong Kong (teaching an ESL class), and Charles Lewis of Mesa Community College, in the United States (teaching business English), organized a project focusing on the environment for students in their courses (see Vilmi, n.d., http://www.hut.fi/~rvilmi/autumn94/environment.html). Via e-mail, students worked in international teams of approximately eight students to find the best solution for a real-world environmental problem. The teachers established an e-mail list to discuss the aims of the project and set the tasks and schedule. Each student team also had its own e-mail list for communication and collaboration.

Each group selected an environmental problem from a list of suggestions, including nuclear power, wildlife preservation, noise pollution, groundwater contamination, and exhaust pollution. Each group completed and submitted a written portfolio consisting of an introductory letter or CV, a report stating the importance of the problem, a 3-year plan for tackling the problem, a budget outlining what monies would be spent, a technical report recommending solutions to the problem, a 250-word abstract for the Call for Papers for the Fifth International Conference on Improving the Environment, a record of the group's division of labor, and a 250-word essay evaluating the course. Each student submitted the introductory letter or CV and the essay; all the other items were team products.

At the end of the semester, the students gave oral presentations on the work completed in each class; in Finland, other students and teaching staff and members of a sponsoring organization attended the presentations. Students in each class also voted on the best project, and the votes were tabulated so that overall winners could be selected. The students' projects, together with student evaluations, can be found at *Environment Activity* (Vilmi, n.d., http://www.hut.fi /~rvilmi/autumn94/environment.html).

A strength of the project was that it included a number of authentic, collaborative writing assignments in a variety of genres. However, coordinating the project among three different classes with different schedules created difficulties and slowed progress. In the end, students' evaluations of the project were mixed, with some feeling that it had been an exciting learning experience and others frustrated by the complications and delays. The teachers involved are continuing to organize other Internet-based projects in ways that can maximize the strengths of this effort and minimize some of the weaknesses (e.g., by addressing differences of scheduling and expectations during the planning stage).

Conclusion

Although the projects discussed in this chapter were conducted by teachers working in very different circumstances, some common threads are evident. In most cases, Internet-based activity was woven into projects. Students progressed from direct instruction to immersion in project activity and gradually learned to take greater levels of responsibility for their own learning. Neither language nor technology was treated as an end in itself; rather, both were seen as means toward authentic and purposeful communication. The teacher acted as a guide and facilitator, providing sufficient instruction for students to get started, helping the students launch the projects, and supplying additional language or technology support along the way. The final products were not just turned in to the teacher but were also shared with other audiences.

These projects are only a few of the many interesting examples we have come across. There is no single right way to use the Internet in English language teaching, just as there is no one way to use textbooks, tape players, or libraries. However, it is possible to learn from the successes of others, and there is a pattern of positive results being achieved from project-based computer work in the classroom (for more examples, see Cummins & Sayers, 1995; Warschauer, 1995b, 1999).

The Internet is a relatively new medium, and the final chapter on effective use of the Internet in education is far from being written. Without a doubt, you, the readers of this book, will contribute to overcoming the challenges of effectively integrating the Internet in the classroom so that students master the language, technology, and learning skills they need.

Chapter 8

Researching On-Line Language Learning

In this chapter, we discuss approaches to researching language learning in on-line environments and survey research that has been conducted to date.

I s it worthwhile to use the Internet in language teaching? How does language use change in on-line environments? What are the best ways to incorporate e-mail or the World Wide Web into the classroom? You can use several approaches to learn about such issues. One is to talk to fellow teachers. Another is to try things out in the classroom and see how they work. And another is to conduct and share research.

Research has something in common with the second approach, trying things out in the classroom and seeing how they work. The difference is that research is based on a *systematic* investigation. To conduct research is to carefully define questions, decide what kinds of data are needed to answer the questions, plan and implement the collection of data, and analyze the data so as to resolve questions and come to conclusions (see Brown, 1988; Hatch & Lazaraton, 1990; Nunan, 1992). In this chapter, we first briefly address some general questions of approach that relate to all educational research. We then look in more detail at particular approaches to researching the on-line classroom.

Types of Educational Research

The types of educational research fall along the following main continua, among others: experimental versus natural, quantitative versus qualitative, etic versus emic, and product versus process.

EXPERIMENTAL VERSUS NATURAL

Experimental research is based on the goal of trying to find generalizable answers to specific questions. To achieve this, as many variables as possible are held constant so that one or two specific questions can be addressed in tightly controlled experimental situations. According to Larsen-Freeman and Long (1991), "true experiments" (p. 19) must involve two groups, an experiment and a control group, into which subjects have been randomly assigned. A "quasi-experiment" may involve one group that takes a pretest, has some kind of "treatment" (p. 20), and then takes a posttest. In contrast, naturalistic research seeks to understand phenomena in their natural, holistic context. In conducting naturalistic research, instead of controlling outside variables, the researcher attempts to observe and understand how a wide range of contextual factors may be affecting a situation (Lincoln & Guba, 1985).

QUANTITATIVE VERSUS QUALITATIVE

In quantitative research, the data take a numerical form. Quantitative research often makes use of inferential statistics to attempt to demonstrate a statistically significant correlation between two variables. Qualitative research relies on descriptive data that may not be quantified. Some researchers stress the philosophical distinctions between quantitative and qualitative approaches, with quantitative approaches being more positivistic (i.e., trying to prove specific causation based on tightly controlled research) and qualitative research being more holistic (e.g., focusing on understanding events in cultural context; see K. A. Davis, 1995).

ETIC VERSUS EMIC

In etic research, the researcher defines the categories ahead of time and sees whether people's behavior falls into those categories. In emic research, the researcher looks at data and tries to see what kinds of categories emerge from those data based on the meanings and interpretations of the people involved. (Note that the etic-emic distinction is seen in the words *phonetics* and *phonemes*, with the former based on general categories of sounds and the latter based on the meanings of sounds for a particular community.)

PRODUCT VERSUS PROCESS

Product-based research attempts to look at the results of a particular educational situation. Process-based research attempts instead to analyze the processes that take place in the classroom or other learning situations. Often these are combined into process/product research.

ACTION RESEARCH

Action research, another important category, exists not on a continuum but as a type in itself. Action research is research carried out by practitioners in order to improve their own practice. It can involve any of the types of research described above. In action research in education, one or more teachers think about a change they would like to bring about in their classroom. They then develop a plan for (a) introducing the change and (b) investigating the effect of introducing the change. For example, an action research plan for the on-line classroom might involve a teacher's decision to switch from paper journals to e-mail journals. The teacher might try it for 1 month and then compare the new journals to the previous ones to see if students wrote more in the e-mail journals. The teacher might also organize a class discussion or conduct an anonymous survey to find out which kind of journal the students prefer. Following the collection and analysis of the data, the teacher disseminates information to colleagues (e.g., in in-service training sessions, newsletter or journal articles, or informal discussions), makes further curriculum decisions based on what has been learned, and plans a new cycle of action research to continue the learning process (Chamot, 1995).

You can apply any of the above approaches to understanding on-line language learning. In many cases, educational research will fall somewhere between the various approaches. It is important, though, to think about which general approach matches your beliefs and is suitable to address the research questions chosen.

On-Line Language Learning Research

Research conducted to better understand the role of the Internet in language teaching and learning generally involves five overlapping areas: linguistic features, interaction, attitude, context, and language impact.

LINGUISTIC FEATURES

Research that investigates the linguistic features of on-line communication might ask questions such as these: Is e-mail communication more similar to speaking or to writing? What are the lexical, syntactic, and functional features common to on-line communication? Does a unique electronic language exist?

A growing body of first language (L1) research has begun to address these questions. For example, Yates (1996) analyzed samples of computer-mediated communication (CMC) from a British conferencing network with other samples of speech and writing. Measuring *type-token ratio* (i.e., the number of different words [type] compared to the number of total words [token]), he found that CMC lies much closer to the high type-token ratio of writing than the low type-token ratio of speech. On another vocabulary measure, *lexical density* (i.e., ratio of lexical to grammatical items), CMC also lies much closer to writing's high level of lexical density than to the low lexical density of speech. On a third measure, *personal reference* (i.e., the number of second- and third-person pronouns), CMC made much greater use of first- and second-person pronouns than either speech or writing did. Yates concluded that CMC is neither speechlike nor written language–like but has its own distinct features. A similar conclusion was arrived at by Collot and Belmore (1996), who analyzed a large sample of language in a synchronous computer conference in relation to dimensions of speech and writing defined by Biber (1988).

Some of the linguistic characteristics of CMC might be important for language learning. The frequent use of first- and second-person pronouns suggests a personal form of writing that may be nonthreatening for the writer, and the high degree of lexical density suggests a good environment for pushing language development forward.

Research on these questions in second language (L2) environments is more limited. In one oft-cited study of students of English using Daedalus InterChange (a component of the software Daedalus Integrated Writing Environment, 1997), Warschauer (1996a) found the type-token ratio of CMC for students using the software to be significantly higher than the type-token ratio of the same students in speech. Similarly, he found syntactic complexity (measured by comparing the number of dependent clauses to the total number of clauses) to be significantly greater in CMC than in speech.

Biesenbach-Lucas, Weasenforth, and Meloni (1998) compared students' writing of texts in an on-line mode (while connected to the Internet using the e-mail software Pine, 1996) and in an off-line mode (using the word-processing software WordPerfect, 1997). They found that the elements of textual cohesion of the two types of text were quite similar but that students wrote longer texts in the off-line mode.

Finally, the differences among the interface used in various forms of CMC also affect language use. A number of studies have pointed to the special characteristics of Internet-based chat, such as brevity, abbreviation, and use of paralinguistic cues (e.g., "ba-a-a-ad"; Werry, cited in Moran & Hawisher, 1998, p. 96) found in text produced with chat software such as ICQ (1999) and Internet Relay Chat, but these linguistic characteristics are generally found less frequently in communication via e-mail or Daedalus InterChange.

Although work on the linguistic characteristics of L2 communication is just beginning, this area will surely be an important one for research in the future. The fact that on-line language is de facto electronically archived, and thus need not be transcribed or scanned, makes it relatively easy to analyze. A number of analytical tools, such as the Child Language Data Exchange System (CHILDES) (MacWhinney, 1995; see http://childes.psy.cmu.edu), can aid linguistic analysis. One resource that researchers in this area will find invaluable is Wolfe-Quintero, Inagaki, and Kim's (1998) book, which contains an exhaustive list of measures used to evaluate fluency, accuracy, and complexity in L2 writing.

INTERACTION

Another important body of research investigates the nature of on-line interaction: How do people negotiate in CMC? What kind of turn-taking rules apply? What kinds of participation patterns are typical? Some clear patterns are beginning to emerge from the L1 and L2 studies conducted on these questions.

First, in many-to-many computer-assisted conversation, there is much greater equality of participation than in oral class discussion. Specifically, the computer-assisted conversation is less dominated by the instructor, the teacher takes relatively fewer turns, and the students direct most of their comments to each other rather than to the teacher (Chun, 1994; Kern, 1996). In addition, the turns are more equally distributed among the students; shy students participate more, and a small number of assertive students dominate less often than in face-to-face conversation (Kelm, 1995; Kern, 1995b; Sullivan & Pratt, 1996; Warschauer, 1996a).

Another often-noted feature of computer-assisted conversation is that it disrupts what might be considered normal rules of turn taking because a number of people can be writing at once. This feature undoubtedly contributes to the more equal distribution of participation noted above, but it can also result in a series of asocial monologues rather than in interactive discussion. Pinto (1996), for example, analyzing English language students' discussion on a MOO, found that the majority of conversational turns consisted of initiating moves (e.g., initial statements or questions) rather than responding, reacting, or extending moves. This situation may be less acute in asynchronous communication, such as e-mail, in which the slower exchange may facilitate more direct response and idea building (Kern, 1996).

Turn taking in one-to-one CMC does seem to foster dialogue either in synchronous (Kroonenberg, 1995) or in asynchronous mode (St. John & Cash, 1995). What's more, CMC has been found to foster substantial negotiation of meaning, resulting in linguistic modifications toward more targetlike use of language (Pelletieri, 2000). This appears to be especially true when challenging tasks require learners to request and obtain information from each other for successful completion (Pelletieri, 2000).

Whether in one-to-one (see St. John & Cash, 1995) or many-to-many (see Warschauer, 1999) format, CMC appears to give students a rich repertoire of language chunks to notice, analyze, save, and incorporate into their own language production, thus heightening their ability to learn from others' language use.

ATTITUDE

A third area of research has investigated students' attitude toward using the Internet in the language classroom: Does use of the Internet increase students' motivation? Do certain types of Internet-based activities affect attitude differently than others do? Does the Internet have a different impact on the attitude of different types of students?

Warschauer (1996b) conducted a survey of L2 students using the Internet for writing and communication in 12 university courses in three countries. A high degree of motivation was associated with the use of computers and the Internet in all the courses, with little difference between ESL and EFL classrooms. A factor analysis revealed three main factors affecting students' motivation: (a) their interest in authentic communication, (b) the amount of personal power and control that they felt mastering computers and the Internet gave them, and (c) the perceived positive impact of computer mastery on their learning and achievement. In this study, the greatest degree of motivation occurred in classrooms where the teachers had integrated Internet-based activities into the curriculum rather than using computers in a peripheral fashion. Other qualitative studies (e.g., Warschauer, 1999) and action research studies (Barson, Frommer, & Schwartz, 1993) have shown similar results. An in-depth study by Tella (1992a) indicated that the positive effect on attitude extends to both female and male high school students, with girls drawing in large measure on their interest in writing and interpersonal communication and boys drawing in part on their general positive attitude toward working with computers and other electronic equipment.

The studies mentioned above largely focused on the use of e-mail or the World Wide Web for long-distance communication. When on-line communication has principally been used for in-class conversation, students' motivation has not been as uniformly high (Meunier, 1998).

CONTEXT

A fourth area of research examines the context of on-line learning: How does the sociocultural context of the learning situation, including the teachers' and students' backgrounds and beliefs and the nature of the educational institution and community, affect the processes and results of on-line learning? Do some teaching contexts or approaches seem more congruent with successful incorporation of the Internet than others do?

Research on context has relied on qualitative observation in the form of case studies (Meskill & Krassimira, 2000), action research (Barson et al., 1993), and ethnography (e.g., Warschauer, 1998a, 1999). A substantial body of research (see, e.g., Barson et al., 1993; Meskill & Krassimira, 2000; Tella, 1992b) has found that the integration of on-line technology can have positive effects when teachers and their institutions are open to educational reform and, in particular, to devolving more power to students. In these situations, the integration of information and communications technology has resulted in increased collaborative learning, more student autonomy, and a more communicative curriculum focused on authentic interaction. On the other hand, when teachers or institutions have been resistant to student-centered learning, results have been poor, as the students view computer activities as another form of teacher-mandated busy work (Warschauer, 1998a).

Students from a wide range of sociocultural backgrounds seem to benefit from Internet-based activity. Using the Internet can be especially effective for students from cultural groups that value hands-on learning, the use of visual media, and the forging of connections with the community (Warschauer, 1998b).

LANGUAGE IMPACT

Another area of research attempts to assess the impact of on-line activity on students' postactivity language use: Do students measurably improve in language proficiency as a result of their time spent on-line?

Case studies have attempted to document students' language improvement resulting from on-line activity (see, e.g., St. John & Cash, 1995), but this is a challenging area of research, as it is often difficult to sort out how much improvement is due to having used the Internet and how much is due to other language learning activities. One particular area of research has looked at the impact of CMC on students' subsequent writing. In Sullivan and Pratt's (1996) study, a group that studied writing using computer-assisted conversation improved more in their writing ability from the beginning to the end of a semester than a control group that used face-to-face conversation. Schultz (2000) looked specifically at how language learners incorporated feedback into their writing following peer review sessions conducted via Daedalus InterChange and via face-to-face discussion. She found that the students using Daedalus InterChange incorporated more of the specific suggestions made by their peers, whereas the group using face-to-face discussion made more global changes. The best results were achieved with groups that were allowed to alternate the use of Daedalus InterChange and face-to-face discussion for peer review.

Conclusion

We hope that the references cited in this chapter provide a useful starting point for readers interested in conducting research on on-line learning. Of course, a good deal of information on this topic is also available on the Internet. For an example of action research on on-line language teaching, see Shetzer (1997, http://www.newtierra.com/shetzer97). Links to a number of the articles mentioned in this chapter are available on Mark Warschauer's home page (http://www.lll.hawaii.edu/web/faculty/markw). Research reviews available on-line include *Processes and Outcomes in Networked Classroom Interaction* (Ortega, 1997, http://polyglot.cal.msu.edu/llt/vol1num1) and *Computer-Mediated Collaborative Learning: Theory and Practice* (Warschauer, 1997, http://www.lll.hawaii.edu/web/faculty/markw/cmcl.html). The current issue and archives of *Language Learning & Technology* (http://polyglot.cal.msu.edu/llt) contain numerous examples of excellent research on the topic. Finally, also worth consulting is *Computer-Mediated Communication in Foreign Language Education: An Annotated Bibliography* (Coski & Kinginger, 1996, http://www.lll.hawaii.edu/nflrc/NetWorks/NW3).

The Internet is a young medium, and research in this area is just beginning. Relatively few studies have been published on synchronous and asynchronous CMC in language learning, and fewer still have been published on the use of the World Wide Web. The research conducted to date does not yield any simplistic conclusions about the Internet being de facto superior to other media or means for language learning. Indeed, it would be foolhardy to expect such a far-reaching conclusion, as the Internet is a medium rather than a method, and as such it can be deployed toward useful and less useful ends. Research studies in this area will likely yield not general conclusions but rather specific insights into the impact of using particular on-line activities in particular circumstances. An accumulation of such specific insights over time, however, may allow us as teachers to continually improve our understanding of the role of the Internet in English teaching.

Research on on-line language learning may eventually serve broader purposes than providing pedagogical guidance. The large amount of L2 interaction occurring on-line, and the ease with which this interaction can be electronically archived and analyzed, makes on-line communication a potentially important source for investigating a wide range of issues related to L2 acquisition and use. In due time, the power of computers and the Internet may help us not only increase our understanding of the on-line classroom but also unlock broader mysteries of the language learning process.

Supplement:
How to Make Web Pages

T his guide will give you the information you need to make basic World
Wide Web pages for your class and to help your students make pages. If
you are interested in developing intermediate or advanced pages, you will
also find information of value as well as pointers to further resources.

Creating Web pages and offering them on the Internet usually involves two
steps: (a) creating the pages and saving them to the hard drive of your computer
(or on a diskette) and (b) putting the pages on an Internet-accessible server. This
supplement discusses

1. the creation of basic Web pages with Hypertext Markup Language
   (HTML) and a variety of software
2. the addition of multimedia, including images, audio, and video, to Web
   pages
3. other elements of Web pages, such as forms and discussion boards
4. options for storing Web pages on Internet servers
5. the issues of intellectual property, copyright, and plagiarism

Web Page Basics

Web pages are documents that are stored on the Internet. They are usually text
files coded in HTML, which consists of various *tags* that enable Web pages to be
displayed with the same layout on different computers. For example, Figure 1
displays the HTML coding used in a fictitious Grammar 101 Web page, which
is shown in Figure 2. The HTML tags in Figure 1, which are enclosed in " < >,"
tell the Web browser (e.g., Netscape Communicator, 1999, or Microsoft Internet
Explorer, 1999) how to format or lay out the content of the Grammar 101 Web
page so that computers around the world will see the information in a uniform

fashion. When users look at the Web page, however, they do not see what is shown in Figure 1; rather, they see the resulting Web page, shown in Figure 2.

Web pages might contain connections called *links*—dynamic words, phrases, or objects. When users click the mouse on a link, they are taken to a different Web page or location on the Web. The Grammar 101 Web page in Figure 2 has two links, one leading to a course syllabus and another leading to a page called *Grammar Links*. A collection of Web pages that are connected together by links is called a *Web site*. Web sites can include *internal links*, which connect to pages stored locally (i.e., on the same computer or server, as in the Grammar 101 Web page), and *external links*, which connect to pages stored on servers other than the one used by the Web author. The main page of the Web site is known as a *home page*.

TO HTML OR NOT TO HTML?

In the early 1990s, the only way to make a Web page was to learn HTML. Developed by the World Wide Web Consortium (http://www.w3.org), HTML continues to evolve and change, allowing Web authors a wider range of expression. The only reason to learn about HTML coding, however, is to be able to develop complex features for Web pages without the assistance of a specialist. If you or your students are in this category, consult the HTML resources in Resource Guide 1. A recent development in the rapidly changing technology of

Figure 1. HTML Coding for Grammar 101 Web Page

```
<HTML>
<HEAD>
<TITLE>Grammar 101</TITLE>
</HEAD>

<BODY>
<H1>Grammar 101</H1>
<P>
This Web page is home to the Grammar 101 course for
Summer quarter 2000. It contains the syllabus for the
course, as well as links to helpful grammar sites on
the Web.
<P>
<A HREF="syllabus.html">Syllabus</A>
<P>
<A HREF="links.html">Grammar Links</A>
</BODY>
</HTML>
```

Figure 2. Grammar 101 Web Page in Internet Explorer

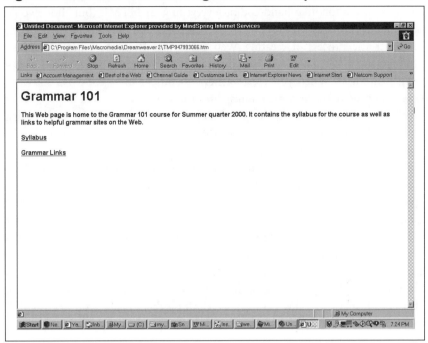

Web page coding is Extensible Markup Language (XML), which "enables designers to create their own customized tags to provide functionality not available with HTML. For example, XML supports links that point to multiple documents, as opposed to HTML links, which can reference just one destination each" (*Webopedia,* http://www.webopaedia.com, s.v. "XML," July 22, 1999).

Resource Guide 1: HTML

- *Extensible Markup Language (XML)* (Connolly, 1997): http://www.w3.org/XML
- *How to Create a Basic Web Page With HTML* (Shetzer, 1999a): http://www.newtierra.com/tags.html
- *HTML Goodies:* http://www.htmlgoodies.com
- *HTML Home Page* (Raggett & Jacobs, 1997): http://www.w3.org/MarkUp
- *HTML: An Interactive Tutorial for Beginners* (Kristula, 1999): http://www.davesite.com/webstation/html
- The World Wide Web Consortium: http://www.w3.org

SOFTWARE FOR CREATING WEB PAGES

Some Web authors like hand-coding everything in HTML, but most would rather focus primarily on the content of their pages and use software that greatly simplifies the process of creating Web pages (see Resource Guide 2). These products use a *WYSIWYG* ("what you see is what you get"; pronounced "wizzy whig") interface. When you create a new document in WYSIWYG software, what you type onto the screen looks almost exactly like the final display in the Web browser. In contrast, creating a Web page directly in HTML involves first typing codes into a text editor (as seen in Figure 1) and then viewing the file using a Web browser (as in Figure 2).

Basic Web pages can be created quite easily with free software such as Netscape Composer, a component of Netscape Communicator (1999). You can download the software free of charge or purchase a CD-ROM installation disk for a minimal fee—a good idea if a slow or unreliable Internet connection makes it difficult for you to download the software. You can also create basic Web pages with word-processing software, such as Microsoft Word (1999), by typing a file and saving it as an HTML document. Several commercial packages, such as Dreamweaver (1999) and Microsoft FrontPage (1999), allow the incorporation of some advanced WYSIWYG features. Both products enable you to create fill-in forms and button rollovers (the effect that changes the color of a button when the user moves the mouse over it).

When selecting software to use for creating Web pages, first do some research to see whether the capabilities and price of the software match your needs and resources. If you work for an educational institution, be sure to investigate buying the software at a discount, and ask others at your institution what software they are using. When purchasing computer hardware or software to use at home, consider buying the same software that you use in the institutional computer lab so you can easily move files back and forth. Many software companies offer demo versions of software that you can download from

Resource Guide 2: Software for Creating Web Pages

- Adobe GoLive (1999): http://www.adobe.com/products/golive/main.html
- Adobe PageMill (1999): http://www.adobe.com/products/pagemill/main.html
- Dreamweaver 3 (1999): http://www.dreamweaver.com
- Home Page (1999): http://www.claris.com/products/hp_home.html
- Microsoft FrontPage (1999): http://www.microsoft.com/frontpage
- Microsoft Word (1999): http://www.microsoft.com/office/word
- NetObjects Fusion (1998): http://www.netobjects.com
- Netscape Communicator (Composer) (1999): http://home.netscape.com

a Web site and try out before making a purchasing decision. Institutions that are looking to buy site licenses for a large number of computers should do some careful comparison shopping.

A Multipage Web Site

The possible structures for Web sites vary in level of complexity, layout, and features. Figure 3 shows the structure of a Web site consisting of four Web pages. The main page, or home page, is named *index.html,* and the topic of the entire Web site is *Grammar.* The three Web pages that make up the body of the site are each concerned with a different grammar topic, and the file names have logical relationships to the topics: *object.html, verb.html,* and *subject.html.* The lines drawn between the pages indicate their interconnection.

FILE MANAGEMENT
Creation and Storage
When creating Web sites, it is a good idea to construct the pages off-line (i.e., while you are not connected to the Internet). On the hard drive of your computer or on a diskette, create a folder or directory. Give it the name of the Web site, and store your pages in it. If you create multiple Web sites, save each one in a separate folder or directory. In this way, multiple Web sites are easily distinguishable. In addition, Web sites are easier to conceptualize if you use the same file structures on your hard drive or diskette as will be used on the Web server.

Figure 3. Structure of a Web Site

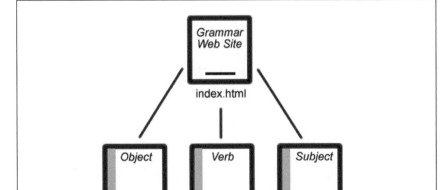

File Extensions

Note that all the file names shown in Figure 3 end with the extension *.html,* the most common file extension for Web pages created on Macintosh computers; the extension *.htm* is commonly found in the file names of pages created on computers running the Microsoft Windows operating system. It doesn't matter which extension is used, and either can be used on either type of computer. If you value consistency, use only one of these extensions within a Web site.

Naming Conventions

Several features of the file names in Figure 3 are worth keeping in mind as you name your Web page files:

1. They are in lowercase letters. Web addresses are case sensitive. If you mix upper- and lowercase letters in file names, future users of your site will face an additional challenge: A user who enters an uppercase letter instead of a lowercase letter, or vice versa, will not reach the Web site. Web authors should strive to make their Web sites easily accessible; using lowercase file names helps.

2. They are relatively short. The longer the file name, the more time it will take future users to type the address of the Web site. Keep file names as compact and as meaningful as possible.

3. There are no spaces between the letters. Browsers have difficulty interpreting spaces in Web page addresses and might substitute a percentage sign (%) for a space.

4. The specific file name *index.html* is used to refer to the main Web page, or home page. Saving the home page with this file name (or, on some Web servers, *default.htm*) gives the Web surfer a shortcut to viewing the Web site. For example, if the complete address of the main page of the Grammar 101 Web site is http://www.newtierra.com/grammar/index .html, typing only http://www.newtierra.com/grammar would take the user to the page.

RELATIVE AND ABSOLUTE LINKS

The links that connect the pages in the sample Grammar 101 Web site are *local,* or *relative,* links (i.e., links to files stored on the same computer), which make it easier to move the Web site to another computer, if necessary. Using relative links also allows easier *off-line browsing,* in which the user views the Web site on a hard drive or a diskette without being connected to the Internet. If your Internet connection is not very stable, you can create Web sites for your students to use off-line. In addition, with software like WebWhacker (1999) or Teleport Pro (1997), you can save a copy of an entire Web site created by someone else and view it later without being connected to the Internet.

In contrast to relative links, *absolute* links are configured to point to the exact location of a Web page on the Internet. A local link to the page called *Object* in Figure 3 would specify only the file named *object.html*, but an absolute link would consist of the exact Web address: http://www.newtierra.com/grammar /object.html. Using absolute links for connecting pages within one's own site is not a good idea, as absolute links depend on an Internet connection in order to function.

Multimedia

In this section, we examine the basics of adding images, audio, and video to Web pages.

IMAGES

Before you add images to Web pages, the files containing the images must be ready to use, must have the appropriate format, and must be saved in the location that is most easily accessible to the Web pages.

File Types: GIF and JPEG

The two standard formats for image files in Web pages are GIF (Graphics Interchange Format, using the extension *.gif*) and JPEG (Joint Photographic Experts Group, using the extension *.jpeg* or *.jpg*). According to Williams and Tollett (1998), GIFs are "best used for images with large areas of solid color, such as simple illustrations, logos, text as graphics, cartoons" (p. 175). JPEGs are better for watercolor, pencil, or charcoal illustrations. The difference between the two formats relates to issues of transparency, interlacing, and animation. In GIF files, the colors can be set to appear transparent whereas the colors in JPEG files cannot. GIFs can be *interlaced* whereas JPEGs cannot. (An interlaced file will load gradually in a browser. It will first appear as a blurry object with the basic size and shape of the image. As it loads, the image will change gradually from blurry to sharp.) Finally, animations are possible with GIF files but not JPEG files.

Web pages contain references to image files; the images are not part of the Web pages. Be sure to save GIF or JPEG files inside the directory or folder set up for the Web site. If you do not, the images might not display on the Web pages when the site is moved to the Internet. Images are stored in a different location on the Web server than Web pages are. If the Web page cannot find the image file, a broken image symbol will be displayed in place of the image (see Figure 4). Also make sure that the names of the image files and the references to those files in the Web pages are identical. If they are not, the images will not show up in the resulting Web page.

Figure 4. Graphics Representing Broken Image Files

Image Size

Remember to keep image files small. The smaller the file, the shorter the load time in the Web browser. Image files are measured in kilobytes and bytes; 1,024 bytes equal 1 kilobyte, and 1,024 kilobytes equal 1 megabyte. To find out the size of images on a computer running Microsoft Windows 95 or 98, look at the contents of the diskette or directory by double-clicking the mouse on its icon within "My Computer." Click once on the image file, and look at the number displayed in the lower right-hand corner of the window. (If the operating system is set to view the contents of directories as Web pages, you might see the file size in the left frame of the window.) To find out the size of a file on a Macintosh computer, open the folder containing the image. Click the mouse on the image once, and select "get info" (Williams & Tollett, 1998).

The size of image files is affected by the dimensions of the image (e.g., how big it appears on the screen) and the density of its resolution. When saving an image for a Web page, do not make it any bigger than necessary; currently most Web authors feel that there is no need to use a resolution greater than 72 dots per inch (dpi).

You can use software to compress image files. Some graphics creation software packages, such as Fireworks 3 (1999) and Adobe ImageReady (a component of Adobe Photoshop, 1999), offer several options for file compression. In addition, several Web sites (e.g., *JPEG Wizard,* http://www.jpegwizard .com; *MediaBuilder GifOptimizer,* http://www.gifoptimizer.com) offer on-line image compression tools. To use these Web-based tools, you must first store the image files on an Internet server so that the tools can access them.

Tables

The best way to control the placement of images on a Web site is to put the images inside a table. For instance, to include an image with writing next to it, as in Figure 5, put the image in one cell of a table and the text in another. To align the top of the text and the top of the image, select that option in the "Row Properties" menu of the software used. You can use table features to vary the layout of images by adding a border so that the table lines are visible, as in Figure 5, or by setting the border for the table at zero so that no table lines appear

Figure 5. Image and Text Placed in Table

Dolphins are common sea creatures to be found in the Santa Barbara area. If you go on a whale watching excursion you're bound to see some dolphins! This picture was taken of a famous dolphin statue created by a local Santa Barbara artist. Its located at the bottom of State Street near the beach.

on the Web page. Using a borderless table is a handy trick for on-line Web page layout, as the lines are visible to you while you create the table but cannot be seen when the resulting page is viewed in the Web browser.

Thumbnails

Thumbnails are miniature displays of image files that can be configured as links. If you want to include several photographs or other images on a Web site, as in a photo gallery or catalogue, the creation of thumbnail images can save bandwidth and allow for a more pleasant Web-browsing experience. Clicking the mouse on a thumbnail takes the user to a larger image file that is especially created for detailed viewing. To create a thumbnail, save the image file twice: first as a small image (the thumbnail) and then in the larger size. Some Web page creation software automates this process.

Obtaining Images

There are several ways to obtain images to use on your Web site:

1. Make them yourself using image creation software (see Resource Guide 3).

2. Take pictures with a digital camera, and download them from the camera directly to the computer with the help of the connection cable and software that come with the camera.

3. Use a scanner to convert photographs and other printed matter, such as drawings and writing, into electronic files, save them in the appropriate file format (e.g., JPEG or GIF), and put them into Web pages. Do not scan and use any copyrighted images; the more original information that is created and shared, the better. If you teach your students how to create Web pages, you should also teach them about copyright regulations. (See the section Intellectual Property, Copyright, and Plagiarism in this supplement.)

Resource Guide 3: Image Creation Software

- Adobe Photoshop (1999): http://www.adobe.com/products/photoshop/main.html
- Fireworks 3 (1999): http://www.macromedia.com/software/fireworks
- GIFSplit (Barchuk, 1997): http://www.jbarchuk.com/gifsplit
- GraphicConverter (1999): http://www.lemkesoft.de
- LView Pro (1999): http://www.lview.com
- Paint Shop Pro (1999): http://www.jasc.com

4. Copy and use images from the many free image banks on the Web (see Resource Guide 4). To download and save a Web image using a computer running Microsoft Windows, click the right-hand mouse button on the image, and choose "save image as." Using a Macintosh computer, download and save an image by clicking the mouse on an image, holding it until a menu pops up, and then choosing "save this image as." Before downloading images from Web sites, check the terms of use so that you do not use somebody else's image or material without permission. When in doubt, ask permission or avoid downloading the material. Again, it is important to discuss these copyright issues in classes where students are making Web pages, as some students might be inclined to copy images without due consideration to copyright matters.

5. Hire a graphic designer. If you want to create a highly polished, customized graphical environment, you might consider this option.

Resource Guide 4: Free Image Banks

- *Animation Factory:* http://www.animfactory.com
- *Background Gallery:* http://www.geocities.com/SoHo/Gallery/6467
- *ClipArtDownload.com:* http://www.clipartdownload.com
- *Clip Art for Web Sites* (2000): http://www.graphicmaps.com/clipart.htm
- *Free Graphics Resources* (2000): http://www.thefreesite.com/freegraphics.htm
- *IconBAZAAR:* http://www.iconbazaar.com
- *3D Webscapes* (Berlin, 1999): http://www.sonic.net/~lberlin/new/3dnscape.html
- *Web Clip Art:* http://Webclipart.miningco.com
- *Windy's Design Studio:* http://www.windyWeb.com
- *ZyGraphics:* http://www.zyris.com

AUDIO

You can add sound to your Web pages in a variety of ways. Whichever method you use, remember that audio files—whether they are MIDI files, files in WAV format, or other music files from cassette tapes or CDs played in a stereo system or CD-ROM drive—are copyrighted. Be sure to obtain permission to use prepared audio files on your Web pages.

Short Sound Files

The easiest way to put a sound file on a Web site is to record the sound through the computer, save it as a file in the appropriate format, and connect it to the Web page with a link. This method is helpful in creating language learning activities that utilize sound, such as those found at *Randall's ESL Cyber Listening Lab* (http://www.esl-lab.com). The site also contains helpful tutorials on adding sound to Web pages.

To create sound files, you need specialized software. On a Macintosh computer, you can record basic files using Ultra Recorder (Campbell, 1998) or the free SoundRecorder (Jenny, 1998). On a computer running Microsoft Windows 95 or 98, you can use the multimedia accessory Microsoft Sound Recorder. A browse through the audio section of *Download.com* (http://www.download.com), *Shareware.com* (http://shareware.cnet.com), or *Tucows Network* (http://www.tucows.com) will reveal several other software packages for preparing audio files for the Web.

Other sound files of interest are MIDI (Musical Instrument Digital Interface) files. When played, these instrumental music files sound like computer beeps rather than like actual musical instruments. They can be created with MIDI software, such as Anvil Studio (1999) and other products listed in "MIDI for the Masses" (Morris, 1999).

Streaming Audio Files

To prepare longer audio files for the Internet, you need software that encodes sound files into streaming audio files. RealNetworks offers RealProducer Plus (1999), which is helpful for preparing streaming files in RealAudio format. Apple's QuickTime 4 Pro (1999) also allows the creation of streaming audio files in a multitude of formats. Another format to consider is Microsoft's Windows Media Technologies (1999), which boasts the delivery of "FM-stereo-quality streaming audio for all modem users" (*Microsoft Announces Beta Release,* 1999). To learn more about the creation of these types of files, see Resource Guide 5.

Another way to incorporate audio and other streaming multimedia (such as animations) into Web sites is through the use of Shockwave content created with Macromedia's Director (1999). Shockwave technology allows several advanced features, such as the integration of audio files with user interaction. *Cutting Edge CALL Demos* (Duber, 1999) contains several sophisticated examples using

Resource Guide 5: Audio and Video Resources

Web Sites and Documents

- *Cutting Edge CALL Demos* (Duber, 1999): http://www-writing.berkeley.edu /chorus/call/cuttingedge.html
- "MIDI for the Masses" (Morris, 1999): http://www.wdvl.com/Multimedia /Sound/Audio/midi.html
- *QuickTime VR Authoring* (2000): http://www.apple.com/quicktime/qtvr
- *Randall's ESL Cyber Listening Lab:* http://www.esl-lab.com
- *Web Developer's Virtual Library:* http://www.wdvl.com

Software

- Anvil Studio (1999): http://www.AnvilStudio.com
- Director (1999): http://www.macromedia.com/software/director
- QuickTime 4 Pro (1999): http://www.apple.com/quicktime/authoring
- RealProducer Plus (1999): http://www.realnetworks.com/products/producerplus
- Shockwave Player (1999): http://www.macromedia.com/shockwave/download
- SoundRecorder (Jenny, 1998): http://dgrwww.epfl.ch/~jenny
- Ultra Recorder (Campbell, 1998): http://members.aol.com/ejc3/Ultra.html
- Windows Media Technologies (1999): http://www.microsoft.com/windows /windowsmedia

Shockwave technology, such as listening comprehension demo activities in the form of minimal pairs. In these activities, the user listens to and distinguishes the minimal pairs by playing the fast, high-quality audio files and then clicking the mouse on the word played. Users receive feedback on the site and results by e-mail.

Plug-ins

Accessing some audio and video files on the Web requires the use of a browser *plug-in,* "a hardware or software module that adds a specific feature or service to a larger system" (*Webopedia,* http://www.webopaedia.com, s.v. "plug-in," July 21, 1999). At Netscape's *Browser Plug-ins* (http://www.netscape.com/plugins), for instance, you can download plug-ins for playing audio, video, and animation files in formats such as RealAudio, Shockwave, and Flash. Plug-ins for other browsers (e.g., Microsoft Internet Explorer) can be found on the browser companies' sites.

VIDEO

To include video on your Web site, you need a digitized video file that can be encoded into the proper format for on-line delivery. You can create a streaming video file using the tools mentioned in the Audio section, such as RealProducer Plus (1999), Apple's QuickTime 4 Pro (1999), or Microsoft's Windows Media Technologies (1999). Keep in mind that, like audio files, video files take up a large amount of space on the Web server.

A simulated role play called "My Apartment: The Game," found at *Cutting Edge CALL Demos* (Duber, 1999), is an interesting example of the use of QuickTime VR technology, RealAudio streaming sound technology, and the JavaScript programming language. The scenario is as follows. By means of a QuickTime VR movie, the user visits the author's virtual apartment and wants something to drink. The author asks the user a question that includes the phrase *on the rocks*. To find the answer to the author's question, the user must look around the apparently three-dimensional apartment scene by clicking the mouse through the movie. When the user clicks on various parts of the movie, a text box displays feedback. This multimedia language learning simulation combines navigable video, audio, user action, and program response in text form.

For information on preparing video files for Web sites that is beyond the scope of this supplement, see the listings in the Resource Guide 6.

Other Web Page Elements

Besides text, graphics, audio, and video, you can include other interactive components on your Web pages that serve various purposes, such as gathering information from users, structuring class discussions, and organizing information.

FORMS AND ON-LINE QUIZZES

Forms are useful for collecting information from users for a variety of purposes: on-line needs analyses, assignments, feedback, and surveys. Forms contain a variety of elements, such as text boxes for typed words and sentences, and check boxes and radio buttons for on-line quizzes. Figure 6 shows an excerpt from an

---

Resource Guide 6: Web Developer Forums

- *CNET Builder.com:* http://builder.cnet.com
- *WebDeveloper.com:* http://www.Webdeveloper.com
- *Web Developer's Journal:* http://Webdevelopersjournal.com
- *Webmonkey:* http://www.hotwired.lycos.com/Webmonkey
- *WebReference.com:* http://www.Webreference.com

Figure 6. Radio Buttons on an On-Line Form

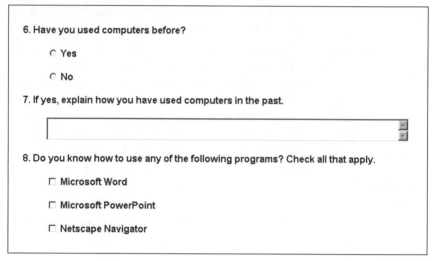

6. Have you used computers before?

    ○ Yes

    ○ No

7. If yes, explain how you have used computers in the past.

8. Do you know how to use any of the following programs? Check all that apply.

    □ Microsoft Word

    □ Microsoft PowerPoint

    □ Netscape Navigator

on-line needs analysis form used in a course on computer-assisted language learning. Note that Question 6 contains radio buttons, Question 7 contains a text box, and Question 8 contains check boxes. You can create forms by writing them directly in HTML or by using software such as Dreamweaver 3 (1999), Microsoft FrontPage (1999), or Adobe PageMill (1999).

Creating the form is only part of the procedure necessary to collect and process user input through a Web page. Forms can work in conjunction with common gateway interface (CGI) scripts that process the data entered by the user. CGI scripts are stored in the CGI-bin directory of the Web server (a server-side solution). Forms can also work with scripts written in JavaScript, which are embedded within the coding of the Web page (a client-side solution).

CGI Scripts

CGI scripts usually work on a wider range of browsers than JavaScript sequences do. A disadvantage of CGI scripts is that they require a live Internet connection in order to function. Moreover, the learning curve for writing CGI scripts is steep even for the experienced Web coder. However, learning how to use and manipulate CGI scripts written by others is not difficult; see Resource Guide 7 for some that can be used in Web sites.

If you want highly customized scripts or prefer not to delve into the intricacies of this matter, consider hiring a programmer. Another option is to use Web-based CGI scripts (see Resource Guide 8), which let you use a CGI application stored on someone else's Web server (but note that some of these come with built-in advertisements). For further information about CGI scripts, see the CGI section of *New Tierra*'s links (http://www.newtierra.com/links).

Resource Guide 7: Free and Shareware CGI Scripts

Collections on the Web

- *The CGI Collection*: http://www.itm.com/cgicollection
- *The CGIemail Home Page*: http://Web.mit.edu/wwwdev/cgiemail
- *Matt's Script Archive*: http://worldwidemart.com/scripts
- *Scripts for Educators* (Pfaff-Harris, 1996): http://www.linguistic-funland .com/scripts
- *The Scripts Home*: http://www.virtualcenter.com/scripts2
- *WebScripts* (Burgdorf, 2000): http://awsd.com/scripts
- *Web Scripts: Examples for Language Learning* (Godwin-Jones, 1998): http://www.fln.vcu.edu/cgi/archive.html

Individual Software Packages

- Links 2.0 (1999): http://www.gossamer-threads.com/scripts
- Tango for Filemaker Pro (1997): http://www.everyware.com

JavaScript Sequences

The JavaScript programming language is not as powerful as CGI but is easier to use. For quizzes created with JavaScript, see *Self-Study Quizzes for ESL Students* (1999, http://www.aitech.ac.jp/~iteslj/quizzes/index.html), a section of *The Internet TESL Journal*. The Internet TESL Journal also contains easy-to-follow instructions for creating on-line quizzes (see *Self-Study Quizzes for ESL Students Project*, 1999, http://www.aitech.ac.jp/~iteslj/quizzes/project.html). Another useful tool for developing JavaScript pages is the freeware package Hot Potatoes (1999), which enables you to create on-line crossword puzzles, gap-fills, scrambled sentences, and other quizzes.

DISCUSSION BOARDS

To hold an on-line, asynchronous discussion on your Web site, you can set up a threaded discussion board using a CGI script. The discussion will be organized in a hierarchical manner (see, e.g., *ESL Discussion Center*, Sperling, 2000, http://

Resource Guide 8: Web-Based CGI Scripts

- *Ed Tech Tools: Free On-Line Services for Educators*: http://motted.hawaii.edu
- *Freedback.com*: http://www.freedback.com
- QuizMaker 2.0 Demo (Shadian, 1997): http://www.mrtc.org/~twright/quizzes /quizcenter/makerdemo.html

Resource Guide 9: CGI Scripts for On-Line Discussion

- Everychat (1999): http://www.everysoft.com/everychat
- WebBBS (1999): http://awsd.com/scripts/webbbs

www.eslcafe.com/discussion). Threaded discussion boards can be used either as a supplementary component of a traditional on-line course or as a principal form of discussion in a distance education course. See Resource Guide 9 for several CGI scripts for on-line discussion that are available free or for a fee.

Sites such as Nicenet's *Internet Classroom Assistant* (http://www.nicenet.org) and *Blackboard* (http://www.blackboard.com) offer you another way to set up threaded discussion, create on-line quizzes, and develop pages for sharing links and documents. To use these tools effectively, you and your students will require a stable Internet connection. Resource Guide 10 contains additional options for the creation of on-line class sites for distance learning.

DATABASES AND SEARCH ENGINES

As mentioned in chapter 4, one exciting use of Web sites is to compile author-driven or user-driven databases of information that are accessible by means of a series of links. This development marks a move from the traditional library organized by librarians to the personal library organized by individuals or organizations. Gossamer Threads' Links Manager 2.0 (1999), a CGI script, enables users to manage and edit a linked database through a Web page interface. Links can be organized by topic and subtopic, and the links can be automatically checked (i.e., to see whether a link still reaches another site or is "dead"). Also included is a component that can send e-mail to users who submit a link to the collection. Links Manager 2.0 is quite useful for creating and maintaining on-line knowledge centers designed to organize an individual's own research results or research collected with specific users in mind. The database of links at *New Tierra* (http://www.newtierra.com), for example, was created with Links Manager 2.0.

Resource Guide 10: Web Courseware Packages

- *Blackboard:* http://www.blackboard.com
- Nicenet's *Internet Classroom Assistant:* http://www.nicenet.org
- Remote Technical Assistance (1999): http://escher.cs.ucdavis.edu:1024
- *Speakeasy Studio and Café:* http://morrison.wsu.edu/studio

Storing Web Pages

To make your Web page publicly available throughout the Internet—that is, to allow other people to view it on-line—you must store it on an Internet-accessible Web server. There are several options for finding space on a Web server. First, universities, colleges, and schools often provide educators with free Web space. Second, if you have a dial-up Internet account with an Internet service provider (ISP) at home, check to see whether your regular service includes Web server space. Also investigate the possibility of renting server space from an ISP; look at advertisements in computer magazines.

A number of Web sites offer free Web space in exchange for the use of personal information for advertising purposes (see Resource Guide 11). They usually require you to display advertisements, watermarks, and other promotional matter furnished by the Web provider or its advertisers within the content of the Web pages. These promotional devices are configured automatically at the server level. One problem with this option is that you cannot control the content of the information in the ads. If you fundamentally disagree with a product or service advertised, you might need to move your Web site elsewhere. On the other hand, these sites offer access to tools that help make ideas available to others on the Internet, and that in itself is reason enough to consider their use, especially if no other publishing option is available. Always make sure to read the legal documents on the Web site, often called *terms of use,* before clicking the "accept" button on the Web space provider's user agreement.

Finally, if you have access to fast Internet connections and the technical knowledge required, you might set up your own server, especially in a university or commercial context. You can discuss this option with the personnel in the computer department at your institution.

UPLOADING WEB PAGES
Once you have located space on a Web server, you will have to upload your pages from your computer diskette or hard drive onto the Web server. How you do this depends on the type of software used to create the Web pages as well as the location and type of Web server. Check with the provider of the Web server space

---

Resource Guide 11: Free Web Space

- *The Free Webpage Provider Review:* http://fwpreview.ngworld.net
- *Tripod:* http://www.tripod.lycos.com
- *XOOM.com:* http://xoom.com
- *Yahoo! GeoCities:* http://www.geocities.yahoo.com

for your options. When you want to update your Web pages, you simply edit the files on your computer and upload them to the Web server once again.

URLs and Domains

Users display Web pages by typing the designated Web addresses (i.e., Uniform Resource Locators, or URLs) into a Web browser. The URL usually indicates the company or organization in charge of the Web site or the Web server, or the name of a product. For example, pages saved at the URL *http://www.xlrn.ucsb.edu* are at the University of California, Santa Barbara Extension, which is an educational organization; hence the end of the URL (*.edu*) specifies an educational domain. If the Web site is a company, the URL ends with *.com*, for commercial domain, as in http://www.netscape.com. Other domains are designated by *.org*, *.net,* and *.gov*. Country codes designate the specific countries in which Web sites are located (e.g., *.jp* for Japan; see Spath, n.d., http://www .bcpl.net/~jspath/isocodes.html).

Domain Name Registration

Domain names are usually registered on-line with an authorized organization. As of April 1999, these organizations were determined by the Internet Corporation for Assigned Names and Numbers (ICANN, http://www.icann.org). ICANN maintains a list of companies from around the world that can register domain names, including Network Solutions (http://www.networksolutions.com) in the United States. Consult ICANN's Web site to find domain registrars within your country. In addition, *Domain Name Registries Around the World* (Norwegian Internet Domain Name Registry, 1999, http://www.uninett.no/navn/domreg .html) contains useful information about this topic.

When registering a domain name, you pay an annual fee in exchange for the right to use the name on the Internet. The name is connected with an Internet Protocol (IP) address, which is a unique number (e.g., the University of California, Santa Barbara's IP address is 128.111.1.1). Before registering a domain name, first check to see if the name is available by doing a search at the domain name registrar's Web site. If the name is available, you also might consider doing a trademark search on the name to see if it has been registered in association with any other commercial or educational project.

Finally, if you would rather not bother with domain name registration yourself, check to see whether your ISP will do it for you. Many ISPs do so as a service for individuals with Web pages located on their server.

Intellectual Property, Copyright, and Plagiarism

Three important issues to keep in mind when making Web sites available on the Internet are intellectual property, copyright, and plagiarism (see Resource Guide 12).

INTELLECTUAL PROPERTY RIGHTS

Intellectual property issues are especially important for educators, as their livelihood often depends on having control over the professional materials and resources they create. To protect their rights, educators are encouraged to read the fine print of contracts with employers, providers of free Web space, and ISPs to ensure that they understand the implications of putting their information on-line and of using the storage method chosen.

Instructors who wish to publish students' writing on their Web sites should get written permission to do so. Students own the writing that they produce, and they should be allowed to control how it is used, including whether or not it is made public on the Internet.

In addition to publishing students' work for them (with their permission), you may want to teach students the skills they need to publish their own Web pages. In that way, students can develop the power to publish, revise, or delete their work from the Internet beyond the scope of the particular course.

COPYRIGHT

According to the World Intellectual Property Organization (WIPO), "copyright protection generally means that certain uses of the work are lawful only if they are done with the authorization of the owner of the copyright" (*International Protection of Copyright and Neighboring Rights,* n.d., http://www.ompi.org/eng /general/copyrght/intro.htm). Images on-line are copyrighted and should not be copied and stored on someone else's Web pages without permission. Structured, organized information in the form of text and links is also copyrighted and should not be copied and placed back on the Internet as someone else's work. Nor should information that is produced and printed on paper, including postcards, magazine pictures, and other professionally created works, be scanned and put on a Web site.

Resource Guide 12: Intellectual Property, Copyright, and Plagiarism

- *Copyright Circulars* (1995): http://lcWeb2.loc.gov/ammem/copcirc.html
- *The Copyright Website:* http://www.benedict.com
- *Plagiarism.org:* http://plagiarism.org
- *World Intellectual Property Organization:* http://www.wipo.org

Students may not be aware of these issues and may see no harm in putting other people's work on their pages. Thus, be sure to discuss the notion of copyright in the classroom and to teach students how to contact the owners of the material in question (e.g., by e-mail) in order to ask permission to use it in an educational project. You can also direct students to the public-access material in the sites listed in Resource Guide 4 above.

PLAGIARISM

Intellectual property and copyright are related to a third important issue, that of plagiarism. Instructors in many countries discourage students from copying information directly from written sources, but the Internet makes it easier for students to copy essays wholesale and turn them in as their own.

Fortunately, though, teachers can easily check to see if work has been plagiarized from the Net. A low-tech solution is simply to take a suspicious phrase from a student's essay, type it into an Internet search engine (in quotation marks), and conduct a search. If you find a phrase that you suspected was plagiarized, you will be able to talk to the student with knowledge of where the material was previously published. A more complete and sophisticated option is to use the services of *Plagiarism.org* (http://plagiarism.org), a site that will check an entire essay for material copied from the Internet. This latter site is commercial but allows a free trial check of up to five manuscripts.

In many academic writing contexts, students are expected to use quotations or paraphrases in their papers and adhere to the quotation and citation format being used in the institution, such as American Psychological Association format or Modern Language Association format (see Resource Guide 13). These guidelines now have rules for citing electronic media, such as Web sites, e-mail addresses, and software, as sources.

In many classrooms, original writing is encouraged and valued. Yet the value of creativity might conflict with other values or beliefs that students have, such as the notion that copying somebody else's words is a good way to learn English or a way to honor the original writer. Dealing with plagiarism in the field of

Resource Guide 13: Citation Formats

- *APA Writing Style Guide* (Borst, 2000): http://www.ldl.net/~bill/apatwo.htm
- *Electronic Reference Formats Recommended by the American Psychological Association* (1999): http://www.apa.org/journals/webref.html
- *MLA Style* (1998): http://www.mla.org/main_stl.htm
- *Publication Manual of the American Psychological Association* (1994): http://www.apa.org/books/pubman.html

TESOL is a complex and important issue, and it is even more so when Web-based publishing is involved. Addressing this issue with students in university settings is especially necessary, as these students may find themselves in circumstances in which borrowing the words of others can have negative consequences.

Although plagiarism is a challenging issue, you can deal with it successfully through honest and sympathetic discussion. We encourage educators to work with students to examine beliefs about how copying and plagiarism are understood in various sociocultural contexts. Using the Internet, you can teach students to point to other sources of information (through links or citations) rather than copy the information directly.

Conclusion

Publishing information on the Web may seem intimidating to a beginner, but it is actually much easier than many people assume. Educators who have taken the time to begin Web publishing projects have for the most part been thrilled by the positive impact such projects have had on their students. Creating and exchanging texts and multimedia documents with people all around the world is an act of wonder. Today's teachers are the first in human history to have the power to do these things. By helping students create and publish their own Web pages—whether their pages consist of just a few paragraphs of text or of sophisticated multimedia presentations—we as teachers are empowering learners to develop new ways to find and express a personal voice.

References

Adobe Acrobat Reader [Computer software]. (1999). Seattle, WA: Adobe Systems. (Available from http://www.adobe.com/products/acrobat/readstep.html)

Adobe GoLive [Computer software]. (1999). Seattle, WA: Adobe Systems. (Available from http://www.adobe.com/products/golive/main.html)

Adobe PageMill [Computer software]. (1999). Seattle, WA: Adobe Systems. (Available from http://www.adobe.com/products/pagemill/main.html)

Adobe Photoshop [Computer software]. (1999). Seattle, WA: Adobe Systems. (Available from http://www.adobe.com/products/photoshop/main.html)

Adult ESL homeownership education. (1999). Washington, DC: Center for Applied Linguistics. Retrieved January 13, 2000, from the World Wide Web: http://www.cal.org/public/fannie.htm.

Advanced English composition online for international students. (1999). Kalamazoo: Western Michigan University. Retrieved January 13, 2000, from the World Wide Web: http://vms.cc.wmich.edu/~kubota/englishonline99.htm.

Ady, J. (1995). Survey across the world. In M. Warschauer (Ed.), *Virtual connections: Online activities and projects for networking language learners* (pp. 101–103). Honolulu: University of Hawai'i, Second Language Teaching and Curriculum Center.

Agre, P. (n.d.). *Red Rock Eater news service.* Retrieved December 13, 1999, from the World Wide Web: http://dlis.gseis.ucla.edu/people/pagre/rre.html.

Alexander, L. G. (1975). *K's first case.* London: Longman.

American Embassy School. (1998). *Endangered animals of India.* New Delhi: Author. Retrieved January 13, 2000, from the World Wide Web: http://cyberfair.gsn.org/falcon/narrative.html.

Anvil Studio [Computer software]. (1999). Shoreline, WA: Willow Software. (Available from http://www.AnvilStudio.com)

AOL Instant Messenger [Computer software]. (1999). Dulles, VA: America Online. (Available from http://www.aol.com/aim)

Arenstein, R. (n.d.). *Webfolios*. Maalot, Israel: Arazim School. Retrieved January 12, 2000, from the World Wide Web: http://www.maltar.org.il/k12/arazim /eng/portfols.htm.

Barchuk, J. (1997). GIFSplit [Computer software]. (Available from http://www .jbarchuk.com/gifsplit)

Barson, J., & Debski, R. (1996). Calling back CALL: Technology in the service of foreign language learning based on creativity, contingency and goal-oriented activity. In M. Warschauer (Ed.), *Telecollaboration in foreign language learning* (pp. 49–68). Honolulu: University of Hawai'i, Second Language Teaching and Curriculum Center.

Barson, J., Frommer, J., & Schwartz, M. (1993). Foreign language learning using email in a task-oriented perspective: Interuniversity experiments in communication and collaboration. *Journal of Science Education and Technology, 4*, 565–584.

BBC schools online. (2000). London: British Broadcasting Corp. Retrieved January 14, 2000, from the World Wide Web: http://www.bbc.co.uk /education/schools.

Beard, R. (1996). *A web of on-line dictionaries*. Retrieved December 12, 1999, from the World Wide Web: http://www.facstaff.bucknell.edu/rbeard /diction.html.

Berlin, L. (1999). *3D Webscapes*. Retrieved January 4, 2000, from the World Wide Web: http://www.sonic.net/~lberlin/new/3dnscape.html.

Biber, D. (1988). *Variations across speech and writing*. Cambridge: Cambridge University Press.

Biesenbach-Lucas, S., Weasenforth, D., & Meloni, C. (1998, March). *On-line vs. off-line texts: The role of medium in determining text variation*. Paper presented at the Annual Conference of the American Association for Applied Linguistics, Seattle, WA.

Boone, S. (n.d.). *World Wide Web scavenger hunt*. Houston, TX: Center for Research on Parallel Computing. Retrieved January 4, 2000, from the World Wide Web: http://www.crpc.rice.edu/CRPC/GT/sboone/Lessons /Titles/hunt/hunt.html.

Borst, W. (2000). *APA writing style guide*. Retrieved January 5, 2000, from the World Wide Web: http://www.ldl.net/~bill/apatwo.htm.

Braunstein, B., Meloni, C., & Zolotareva, L. (1999). *US-SiberLink: An international project linking universities in three cities*. Washington, DC: The George Washington University. Retrieved January 12, 2000, from the World Wide Web: http://www.gwu.edu/~washweb/us-siberlink.htm.

Braunstein, B., Meloni, C., & Zolotareva, L. (2000). US-SiberLink Internet project. *TESL-EJ, 4*(3), A1. Retrieved April 3, 2000, from the World Wide Web: http://ccnic14.kyoto-su.ac.jp/information/tesl-ej/ej15/a1.html.

Brown, J. D. (1988). *Understanding research in second language learning: A teacher's guide to statistics and research design.* Cambridge: Cambridge University Press.

Burgdorf, D. C. (2000). *Webscripts.* Omaha, NE: Affordable Web Space Design. Retrieved January 5, 2000, from the World Wide Web: http://awsd.com /scripts.

Burkhart, L. J. (1999). *Strategies and applications for the one computer classroom.* Retrieved January 12, 2000, from the World Wide Web: http://www .lburkhart.com/elem/strat.htm.

Campbell, E. J. (1998). Ultra Recorder 2.4.1 [Computer software]. EJ Enterprises. (Available from http://members.aol.com/ejc3/Ultra.html)

Catterick, D. (1999, April). *Academic writing and the virtual classroom.* Paper presented at the British Association of Lecturers in English for Academic Purposes Conference, Leeds, England.

Chamot, A. U. (1995). The teacher's voice: Action research in your classroom. *ERIC/CLL News Bulletin, 18*(2), 1, 5–8.

Chun, D. (1994). Using computer networking to facilitate the acquisition of interactive competence. *System, 22,* 17–31.

Clip art for Web sites. (2000). Galveston, TX: Woolwine-Moen Group. Retrieved January 4, 2000, from the World Wide Web: http://www.graphicmaps.com /clipart.htm.

CobuildDirect information. (1999). Birmingham, England: Collins Cobuild. Retrieved December 12, 1999, from the World Wide Web: http://titania .cobuild.collins.co.uk/direct_info.html.

Collins, M., & Berge, Z. L. (2000). *Resources for moderators and facilitators of online discussions.* Berge Collins Associates. Retrieved January 14, 2000, from the World Wide Web: http://www.emoderators.com/moderators.shtml.

Collot, M., & Belmore, N. (1996). Electronic language: A new variety of English. In S. C. Herring (Ed.), *Computer-mediated communication: Linguistic, social, and cross-cultural perspectives* (pp. 13–28). Amsterdam: Benjamins.

CommonSpace (Version 3.5) [Computer software]. (1999). Boston: Sixth Floor Media. (Available from http://www.sixthfloor.com/CS1.html)

Community Learning Center. (n.d.). *Homebuying for everyone.* Boston: Metro Boston Community Wide Education and Information Service. Retrieved January 13, 2000, from the World Wide Web: http://www2.wgbh.org /mbcweis/ltc/final/vvhome.html.

Computer Economics projects worldwide Internet users to approach 350 million by 2005. (1999, January 18). Carlsbad, CA: Computer Economics. Re-

trieved September 1, 1999, from the World Wide Web: http://www
.computereconomics.com/new4/pr/pr990118.html.

Confer V [Computer software]. (1989). Ann Arbor, MI: Advertel Communication Systems.

Confer V beginner's guide. (1989). Ann Arbor, MI: Advertel Communication Systems. Retrieved January 12, 2000, from the World Wide Web: http://www.wmich.edu/docs/3803.html.

Connolly, D. (1997). *Extensible markup language (XML).* World Wide Web Consortium. Retrieved January 4, 2000, from the World Wide Web: http://www.w3.org/XML.

Cook, J. (n.d.). *Janice Cook's English 100.* Honolulu: University of Hawai'i, Kapi'olani Community College. Retrieved May 2, 1999, from the World Wide Web: http://leahi.kcc.hawai.edu.

Copyright circulars. (1995). Washington, DC: Library of Congress. Retrieved January 5, 2000, from the World Wide Web: http://lcWeb2.loc.gov /ammem/copcirc.html.

Corio, R., & Meloni, C. (1995). The Guidelines Net Project. *Computer Assisted English Language Learning, 6*(3), 20–24.

Coski, C., & Kinginger, C. (1996). *Computer-mediated communication in foreign language education: An annotated bibliography* (NetWork #3). Honolulu: University of Hawai'i, Second Language Teaching and Curriculum Center. Retrieved January 10, 2000, from the World Wide Web: http://www.lll.hawaii.edu/nflrc/NetWorks/NW3.

Crystal, D. (1997). *English as a global language.* Cambridge: Cambridge University Press.

Cummins, J., & Sayers, D. (1995). *Brave new schools: Challenging cultural illiteracy through global learning networks.* New York: St. Martin's Press.

CU-SeeMe [Computer software]. (1998). Nashua, NH: White Pine Software. (Available from http://www.wpine.com/Products/CU-SeeMe)

d'Eça, T. A. (n.d.). *The spirit of Christmas.* Retrieved January 12, 2000, from the World Wide Web: http://www.malhatlantica.pt/teresadeca/spiritofxmas.htm.

Daedalus Integrated Writing Environment [Computer software]. (1997). Austin, TX: The Daedalus Group. (Available from http://www.daedalus.com)

Davis, K. A. (1995). Qualitative theory and methods in applied linguistics research. *TESOL Quarterly, 29,* 427–453.

Davis, R. S. (1998a). *Culture Web site project.* Retrieved January 12, 2000, from the World Wide Web: http://www.esl-lab.com/courses/project.html.

Davis, R. S. (1998b). *What's the Internet?* Retrieved January 12, 2000, from the World Wide Web: http://www.esl-lab.com/courses/start.html.

Deguchi, K. (1995). A virtual travel activity in Japanese using the World Wide Web. In M. Warschauer (Ed.), *Virtual connections: Online activities and projects for networking language learners* (pp. 301–303). Honolulu: University of Hawai'i, Second Language Teaching and Curriculum Center.

Director 7 [Computer software]. (1999). San Francisco, CA: Macromedia. (Available from http://www.macromedia.com/software/director)

Directory of online colleges, Internet universities, and training institutes. (2000). Waterbury, VT: Adult Education and Distance Learner's Resource Center. Retrieved January 13, 2000, from the World Wide Web: http://www.geteducated.com/dlsites.htm.

Distance education certificate program. (2000). Madison: University of Wisconsin. Retrieved January 12, 2000, from the World Wide Web: http://uwex.edu/disted/depd/certpro.html.

Distance education online symposium (DEOS). (1999). University Park: The Pennsylvania State University, American Center for the Study of Distance Education. Retrieved January 13, 2000, from the World Wide Web: http://www.ed.psu.edu/acsde/DEOS.html.

Dreamweaver 3 [Computer software]. (1998). San Francisco, CA: Macromedia. (Available from http://www.macromedia.com/software/dreamweaver)

Duber, J. (Ed.). (1999). *Cutting edge CALL demos.* Berkeley: University of California, College Writing Programs. Retrieved January 5, 2000, from the World Wide Web: http://www-writing.berkeley.edu/chorus/call/cuttingedge.html.

Durham, M. (2000, March 24). Google: We're down with ODP. *Salon.com.* Retrieved March 25, 2000, from the World Wide Web: http://www.salon.com/tech/feature/2000/03/24/google_odp/index.html.

East Boston Harborside Community Center. (n.d.). *East Boston Harborside goes to a computer store!* Boston: Metro Boston Community Wide Education and Information Service. Retrieved January 13, 2000, from the World Wide Web: http://www2.wgbh.org/mbcweis/esquare/virtualfront.htm.

Edupage. (n.d.). Boulder, CO: Educause. Retrieved December 13, 1999, from the World Wide Web: http://www.educause.edu/pub/edupage/edupage.html.

Electronic reference formats recommended by the American Psychological Association. (1999, November 19). Washington, DC: American Psychological Association. Retrieved January 5, 2000, from the World Wide Web: http://www.apa.org/journals/webref.html.

E-mail tops telephone, say HR execs at 69th Annual Human Resources Conference. (1998). New York: American Management Association International. Retrieved May 30, 1999, from the World Wide Web: http://www.amanet.org/survey/hrc98.htm.

eMarketer tallies the number of e-mail messages sent in 1999. (1999, February 1). *eStats.* Retrieved May 30, 1999, from the World Wide Web: http://www.emarketer.com/estats/020199_email.html.

English for specific purposes. (1999). Dundee, Scotland: University of Dundee, Centre for Applied Language Studies. Retrieved January 13, 2000, from the World Wide Web: http://www.dundee.ac.uk/languagestudies/esp2 .htm#research.

English Spark Online Magazine. (1996). Hong Kong: City University of Hong Kong, Technical Communications. Retrieved January 20, 2000, from the World Wide Web: http://humanum.arts.cuhk.edu.hk/~cmc/engspark.

Everychat [Computer software] (1999). Midland, MI: Everysoft. (Available from http://www.everysoft.com/everychat)

Faigley, L. (1997). Literacy after the revolution. *College Composition and Communication, 48,* 30–43.

Feenberg, A. (1999). *Distance learning: Promise or threat?* Retrieved May 30, 1999, from the World Wide Web: http://www.rohan.sdsu.edu/faculty /feenberg/TELE3.HTM.

Fireworks 3 [Computer software]. (1999). San Francisco, CA: Macromedia. (Available from http://www.macromedia.com/software/fireworks)

Foelsche, O. (1995). *LLTI listserver.* International Association for Language Learning Technology. Retrieved February 28, 1999, from the World Wide Web: http://iall.net/LLTI.html.

Free graphics resources. (2000). TheFreeSite.com. Retrieved January 4, 2000, from the World Wide Web: http://www.thefreesite.com/freegraphics.htm.

Gaer, S. (1995). Folktales around the world. In M. Warschauer (Ed.), *Virtual connections: Online activities and projects for networking language learners* (pp. 146–148). Honolulu: University of Hawai'i, Second Language Teaching and Curriculum Center.

Gaer, S., & Rosen, D. J. (1999). *A virtual school visit.* Sacramento, CA: Outreach and Technical Assistance Network. Retrieved January 13, 2000, from the World Wide Web: http://www.otan.dni.us/webfarm/emailproject/school.htm.

Godwin-Jones, R. (1998). *Web scripts: Examples for language learning.* Retrieved January 5, 2000, from the World Wide Web: http://www.fln.vcu.edu/cgi /archive.html.

Gralla, P. (2000). Daily double download. *Yahoo! Internet Life.* Retrieved January 19, 2000, from the World Wide Web: http://www.zdnet.com/yil/content /depts/doubledl/dlcurrent/dlcurrent.html.

GraphicConverter [Computer software]. (1999). Peine, Germany: Lemke Software. (Available from http://www.lemkesoft.de)

Gurevich, N. (1995). Teacher-student writing conferences via e-mail. In M. Warschauer (Ed.), *Virtual connections: Online activities and projects for networking language learners* (pp. 211–215). Honolulu: University of Hawai'i, Second Language Teaching and Curriculum Center.

Hatch, E., & Lazaraton, A. (1990). *The research manual: Design and statistics for applied linguistics.* Boston: Heinle & Heinle.

Hess, A. (1995). *Writing around the world—telecommunications and English: The Cities Project.* New York: New York University, American Language Institute. Retrieved December 10, 1999, from the World Wide Web: http://www.nyu.edu/pages/hess/cities.html.

Holliday, L. (n.d.). *CELIA at Latrobe University: Computer enhanced language instruction archive.* Retrieved December 13, 1999, from the World Wide Web: http://www.latrobe.edu.au/www/education/celia/celia.html.

Holliday, L., & Robb, T. (n.d.). *SL-Lists: International EFL/ESL email student discussion lists.* Retrieved January 14, 2000, from the World Wide Web: http://www.latrobe.edu.au/www/education/sl/sl.html.

Home Page [Computer software]. (1999). Santa Monica, CA: Claris. (Available from http://www.claris.com/products/hp_home.html)

Hot Potatoes 4 [Computer software]. (1999). Victoria, Canada: University of Victoria Language Centre, Half-Baked Software. (Available from http://Web.uvic.ca/hrd/halfbaked)

How many online? (n.d.). *Nua Internet Surveys.* Retrieved September 1, 1999, from the World Wide Web: http://www.nua.ie/surveys/how_many_online/index.html.

Hoyle, G. C. (1999). *Colleges and universities.* Retrieved January 13, 2000, from the World Wide Web: http://www.hoyle.com/distance/college.html.

ICQ [Computer software]. (1999). Dulles, VA: ICQ. (Available from http://www.icq.com)

Inspiration (Version 5.0c) [Computer software]. (1997). Portland, OR: Inspiration Software. (Available from http://www.inspiration.com)

International protection of copyright and neighboring rights. (n.d.). Geneva, Switzerland: World Intellectual Property Organization. Retrieved January 1, 2000, from the World Wide Web http://www.ompi.org/eng/general/copyrght/intro.htm.

Isbell, K., & Reinhardt, J. (1998). *Environmental change documentary.* Miyazaki, Japan: Miyazaki International College, Applied Information Science and Environmental Issues. Retrieved January 13, 2000, from the World Wide Web: http://www.miyazaki-mic.ac.jp/classes/fall98/aisenv/projects/project1.html.

Janda, T. (1995). Breaking the ice: E-mail dialogue journal introductions and responses. In M. Warschauer (Eds.), *Virtual connections: Online activities and projects for networking language learners* (pp. 57–58). Honolulu: University of Hawai'i, Second Language Teaching and Curriculum Center.

Jenny, B. (1998). SoundRecorder 1.0 [Computer software]. (Available from http://dgrwww.epfl.ch/~jenny)

Jor, G. (1995). Web newsletter '95: A collaborative learning project for technical writing instruction. In M. Warschauer (Ed.), *Virtual connections: Online activities and projects for networking language learners* (pp. 368–374). Honolulu: University of Hawai'i, Second Language Teaching and Curriculum Center.

Kasper, L. (1999). *CONTENT-ESL.* Retrieved December 10, 1999, from the World Wide Web: http://members.aol.com/Drlfk/Content-ESL.html.

Kelly, C. (1997). How to make a successful ESL/EFL teacher's Web page. *The Internet TESL Journal,* 3(6). Retrieved January 14, 2000, from the World Wide Web: http://www.aitech.ac.jp/~iteslj/Articles/Kelly-MakePage.

Kelm, O. (1995). E-mail discussion groups in foreign language education: Grammar follow-up. In M. Warschauer (Ed.), *Telecollaboration in foreign language learning: Proceedings of the Hawai'i symposium* (pp. 19–28). Honolulu: University of Hawai'i, Second Language Teaching and Curriculum Center.

Kendall, C. (1995). Cyber-surveys. In M. Warschauer (Ed.), *Virtual connections: Online activities and projects for networking language learners* (pp. 97–100). Honolulu: University of Hawai'i, Second Language Teaching and Curriculum Center.

Kenning, M.-M., & Kenning, M. J. (1990). *Computers and language learning: Current theory and practice.* New York: Ellis Horwood.

Kern, R. G. (1995a). Découvrir Berkeley: Students' representation of their world on the World Wide Web. In M. Warschauer (Ed.), *Virtual connections: Online activities and projects for networking language learners* (pp. 355–356). Honolulu: University of Hawai'i, Second Language Teaching and Curriculum Center.

Kern, R. G. (1995b). Restructuring classroom interaction with networked computers: Effects on quantity and quality of language production. *Modern Language Journal,* 79, 457–476.

Kern, R. G. (1996). Computer-mediated communication: Using e-mail exchanges to explore personal histories in two cultures. In M. Warschauer (Ed.), *Telecollaboration in foreign language learning* (pp. 105–119). Honolulu: University of Hawai'i, Second Language Teaching and Curriculum Center.

Kitagawa, M. (n.d.). *Kyoto restaurant project.* Kyoto, Japan: Kyoto Sangyo University. Retrieved January 13, 2000, from the World Wide Web: http://www.kyoto-su.ac.jp/information/restaurant.

Kitagawa, M., Gotou, Y., Saito, N., Sakamoto, T., & Sakane, E. (1997). *Japanese food recipe page.* Kyoto, Japan: Kyoto Sangyo University. Retrieved January 13, 2000, from the World Wide Web: http://www.kyoto-su.ac.jp/information/recipes.

Kitao, K., & Kitao, S. K. (1999a). *Keypal opportunities for students.* Retrieved January 13, 2000, from the World Wide Web: http://ilc2.doshisha.ac.jp /users/kkitao/online/www/keypal.htm.

Kitao, K., & Kitao, S. K. (1999b). *Using TESL-L for research and teaching English.* Retrieved December 10, 1999, from the World Wide Web: http:// www.ling.lancs.ac.uk/staff/visitors/kenji/lis-tesl.htm.

Kristula, D. (1999). *HTML: An interactive tutorial for beginners.* Davesite.com. Retrieved January 4, 2000, from the World Wide Web: http://www .davesite.com/webstation/html.

Kroonenberg, N. (1995). The French connection: Public journals for high school students. In M. Warschauer (Ed.), *Virtual connections: Online activities and projects for networking language learners* (pp. 27–29). Honolulu: University of Hawai'i, Second Language Teaching and Curriculum Center.

Lanham, R. A. (1993). *The electronic word: Democracy, technology, and the arts.* Chicago: University of Chicago Press.

Larsen-Freeman, D., & Long, M. (1991). *An introduction to second language acquisition research.* London: Longman.

Learning resources. (2000). San Francisco: Cable News Network & Western/ Pacific Literacy Network. Retrieved January 14, 2000, from the World Wide Web: http://literacynet.org/cnnsf.

LeLoup, J. W., & Ponterio, R. (1995). *FLTEACH.* Retrieved December 12, 1999, from the World Wide Web: http://www.cortland.edu/flteach.

Lemke, J. L. (1998). Metamedia literacy: Transforming meanings and media. In D. Reinking, M. McKenna, L. Labbo, & R. D. Kieffer (Eds.), *Handbook of literacy and technology: Transformations in a post-typographic world* (pp. 283– 301). Hillsdale, NJ: Erlbaum.

Libweb: Library servers via WWW. (2000). Berkeley: University of California/Sun Microsystems. Retrieved January 12, 2000, from the World Wide Web: http://sunsite.berkeley.edu/Libweb.

Lim, J. (1998). *The one computer classroom.* Berrien Springs, MI: Berrien County Intermediate School District. Retrieved January 12, 2000, from the World Wide Web: http://www.remc11.k12.mi.us/bcisd/classres/onecomp.htm.

Lincoln, Y. S., & Guba, E. G. (1985). *Naturalistic inquiry.* Newbury Park, CA: Sage.

Linkman (Version 2.55) [Computer software]. (1998). Outer Technologies. (Available from http://outertech.com)

Links 2.0 [Computer software]. (1999). Vancouver, Canada: Gossamer Threads. (Available from http://www.gossamer-threads.com/scripts/links)

Livesy, R., & Tudoreanu, E. (1995). "What's yours like? Ours is . . . ." A motivating e-mail project for TESL. In M. Warschauer (Ed.), *Virtual connections: Online activities and projects for networking language learners* (pp.

137–138). Honolulu: University of Hawai'i, Second Language Teaching and Curriculum Center.

LTEST-L. (n.d.). International Language Testing Association. Retrieved December 12, 1999, from the World Wide Web: http://www.surrey.ac.uk/ELI /ltest-l.html.

LView Pro [Computer software]. (1999). Hallandale, FL: MMedia Research. (Available from http://www.lview.com)

MacWhinney, B. (1995). *The CHILDES project: Tools for analyzing talk* (2nd ed.). Mahwah, NJ: Erlbaum.

Mak, L., & Crookall, D. (1995). Project IDEALS: Social interaction and negotiation via cross-cultural simulation. In M. Warschauer (Ed.), *Virtual connections: Online activities and projects for networking language learners* (pp. 205–207). Honolulu: University of Hawai'i, Second Language Teaching and Curriculum Center.

Manteghi, C. (1995). The collaborative fairy tale. In M. Warschauer (Ed.), *Virtual connections: Online activities and projects for networking language learners* (pp. 20–22). Honolulu: University of Hawai'i, Second Language Teaching and Curriculum Center.

Medgyes, P. (1986). Queries from a communicative teacher. *ELT Journal, 40,* 107–112.

Meloni, C. (1995). The cities project. In M. Warschauer (Ed.), *Virtual connections: Online activities and projects for networking language learners* (pp. 211–215). Honolulu: University of Hawai'i, Second Language Teaching and Curriculum Center.

Meloni, C. (1997). Armchair travelers on the information superhighway. In T. Boswood (Ed.), *New ways of using computers in language teaching* (pp. 104–106). Alexandria, VA: TESOL.

Meloni, C. (1998a, January/February). The Internet in the classroom. *ESL Magazine.* Retrieved December 12, 1999, from the World Wide Web: http://www.eslmag.com/Article.htm.

Meloni, C. (1998b, July/August). Language translation on the Web: Fast and free. *ESL Magazine.* Retrieved March 23, 2000, from the World Wide Web: http://www.eslmag.com/netjulaug1998.html.

Meloni, C. (Ed.). (1999). *WOW! Washington on the Web.* Washington, DC: The George Washington University. Retrieved January 10, 2000, from the World Wide Web: http://gwis2.circ.gwu.edu/~gwvcusas/WOWHOME.htm.

Meloni, C. (2000). Wandering the Web. *TESOL Matters.* Retrieved January 14, 2000, from the World Wide Web: http://www.tesol.org/pubs/magz /wanweb.html.

Meloni, C., & Braunstein, B. (Eds.). (1999). *Coast to coast project.* Washington, DC: The George Washington University/University of California, Santa

Barbara. Retrieved January 12, 2000, from the World Wide Web: http:// gwis2.circ.gwu.edu/~gwvcusas/coasttocoast.htm.

Meloni, C., & Miller, L. (1997). *Symposium proceedings: E-mail, the Web, and MOOs: Developing the writing skills of university students in cyberspace.* Washington, DC: Consortium of Universities of the Washington Metropolitan Area. Retrieved December 12, 1999, from the World Wide Web: http://gwis.circ.gwu.edu/~washweb/proceedings.html.

Meskill, C., & Krassimira, R. (2000). Curriculum innovation in TEFL: Technologies supporting socio-collaborative language learning in Bulgaria. In M. Warschauer & R. Kern (Eds.), *Network-based language teaching: Concepts and practice* (pp. 20–40). Cambridge: Cambridge University Press.

Meunier, L. (1998). Personality and motivational factors in electronic networking. In J. Muyskens (Ed.), *New ways of learning and teaching: Focus on technology and foreign language education* (pp. 63–126). Boston: Heinle & Heinle.

Microsoft announces beta release of Windows Media Technologies 4.0 [Press release]. (1999, April 13). Redmond, WA: Microsoft. Retrieved January 5, 2000, from the World Wide Web: http://www.microsoft.com/presspass/press /1999/Apr99/WMT4Betapr.htm.

Microsoft FrontPage 2000 [Computer software]. (1999). Redmond, WA: Microsoft. (Available from http://www.microsoft.com/frontpage)

Microsoft Internet Explorer 5 [Computer software]. (1999). Redmond, WA: Microsoft. (Available from http://www.microsoft.com/windows/IE)

Microsoft NetMeeting [Computer software]. (1999). Redmond, WA: Microsoft. (Available from http://www.microsoft.com/netmeeting)

Microsoft Word 2000 [Computer software]. (1999). Redmond, WA: Microsoft. (Available from http://www.microsoft.com/office/word)

Mills, D. (1999). *Interactive listening comprehension practice.* Carbondale: University of Illinois, Intensive English Institute. Retrieved December 13, 1999, from the World Wide Web: http://deil.lang.uiuc.edu/lcra.

Mills, D., & Salzmann, A. (1999). *Grammar safari.* Carbondale: University of Illinois, Intensive English Institute. Retrieved December 12, 1999, from the World Wide Web: http://deil.lang.uiuc.edu/web.pages/grammarsafari.html.

MLA style. (1998). New York: Modern Language Association. Retrieved January 5, 2000, from the World Wide Web: http://www.mla.org/main_stl.htm.

Moody, S. (n.d.). *NETEACH-L.* Retrieved December 10, 1999, from the World Wide Web: http://www.ilc.cuhk.edu.hk/english/neteach/main.html.

Moran, C., & Hawisher, G. E. (1998). The rhetorics and languages of electronic mail. In I. Snyder (Ed.), *Page to screen: Taking literacy into the electronic era* (pp. 80–101). London: Routledge.

Morris, C. (1999). MIDI for the masses. *Web developer's virtual library.* Retrieved

January 5, 2000, from the World Wide Web: http://www.wdvl.com /Multimedia/Sound/Audio/midi.html.

NetObjects Fusion [Computer software]. (1998). Redwood City, CA: NetObjects. (Available from http://www.netobjects.com)

Netscape Communicator [Computer software]. (1999). Mountain View, CA: Netscape Communications. (Available from http://home.netscape.com /computing/download)

NEW-LIST. (1999). Madison, WI: Internet Scout Project. Retrieved January 20, 2000, from the World Wide Web: http://scout.cs.wisc.edu/scout/caservices /new-list.

The New York Times learning network. (2000). New York: New York Times. Retrieved January 14, 2000, from the World Wide Web: http://www .nytimes.com/learning.

Noble, D. F. (1998). *Digital diploma mills, Part III: The bloom is off the rose.* Retrieved May 30, 1999, from the World Wide Web: http://communication .ucsd.edu/dl/ddm3.html.

Noonan, D. (1999). *LIBCAT: A guide to library resources on the Internet.* Retrieved December 12, 1999, from the World Wide Web: http://www .metronet.lib.mn.us/lc/lc1.cfm.

Norwegian Internet Domain Name Registry. (1999). *Domain name registries around the world.* Trondheim, Norway: NORID. Retrieved January 5, 2000, from the World Wide Web: http://www.uninett.no/navn/domreg.html.

Nunan, D. (1992). *Research methods in language learning.* Cambridge: Cambridge University Press.

Ogbue, U. (1999). *German culture pages in English.* Dresden, Germany: Technische Universität Dresden, Institut für Anglistik/Amerikanistik. Retrieved January 13, 2000, from the World Wide Web: http://www .geocities.com/Athens/Forum/8383.

Online ESL courses. (n.d.). Tower of English. Retrieved January 14, 2000, from the World Wide Web: http://members.tripod.com/~towerofenglish /onlinecourses.htm.

Opp-Beckman, L. (1997). Mysteries that rattle your chains. In T. Boswood (Ed.), *New ways of using computers in language teaching* (pp. 80–81). Alexandria, VA: TESOL.

Ortega, L. (1997). Processes and outcomes in networked classroom interaction: Defining the research agenda for L2 computer-assisted classroom discussion. *Language Learning & Technology, 1*(1), 82–93. Retrieved June 10, 1999, from the World Wide Web: http://polyglot.cal.msu.edu/llt/vol1num1/ortega.

Paint Shop Pro [Computer software]. (1999). Eden Prairie, MN: Jasc Software. (Available from http://www.jasc.com)

Peebles, J. (1996). *Ideas for the one computer classroom.* Madison, WI: Madison

Metropolitan School District, Instructional Technologies. Retrieved January 12, 2000, from the World Wide Web: http://danenet.wicip.org/mmsd-it /tlc/1comprm.html.

Pelletieri, J. (2000). Negotiation in cyberspace: The role of chatting in the development of grammatical competence. In M. Warschauer & R. Kern (Eds.), *Network-based language teaching: Concepts and practice* (pp. 59–86). Cambridge: Cambridge University Press.

Peyton, J. K., & Reed, L. R. (1990). *Dialogue journal writing with nonnative English speakers: A handbook for teachers.* Alexandria, VA: TESOL.

Pfaff-Harris, K. (1996). *Scripts for educators.* Retrieved January 5, 2000, from the World Wide Web: http://www.linguistic-funland.com/scripts.

Pfaff-Harris, K. (1999). *Sites Neteachers thought were cool!* Retrieved December 10, 1999, from the World Wide Web: http://www.linguistic-funland.com /neteach.html.

Pine [Computer software]. (1996). Seattle: University of Washington, Office of Computing & Communications.

Pinto, D. (1996). What does "schMOOze" mean?: Non-native speaker interactions on the Internet. In M. Warschauer (Ed.), *Telecollaboration in foreign language learning: Proceedings of the Hawai'i symposium* (pp. 165–184). Honolulu: University of Hawai'i, Second Language Teaching & Curriculum Center.

Publication manual of the American Psychological Association (4th ed.). (1994). Washington, DC: American Psychological Association. (Available from http://www.apa.org/books/pubman.html)

QuickTime 4 Pro [Computer software]. (1999). Cupertino, CA: Apple Computer. (Available from http://www.apple.com/quicktime/authoring)

QuickTime VR authoring. (2000). Cupertino, CA: Apple Computer. Retrieved January 5, 1999, from the World Wide Web: http://www.apple.com /quicktime/qtvr.

Raggett, D., & Jacobs, I. (1997). *HTML home page.* World Wide Web Consortium. Retrieved January 4, 2000, from the World Wide Web: http:// www.w3.org/MarkUp.

RealPlayer [Computer software]. (1999). Seattle, WA: RealNetworks. (Available from http://www.real.com)

RealProducer Plus [Computer software]. (1999). Seattle, WA: RealNetworks. (Available from http://www.realnetworks.com/products/producerplus)

Reich, R. (1991). *The work of nations: Preparing ourselves for 21st century capitalism.* New York: Knopf.

Remote Technical Assistance [Computer software]. (1999). Davis: University of California. (Available from http://escher.cs.ucdavis.edu:1024)

Rinaldi, A. H. (1998). *Netiquette home page.* Boca Raton: Florida Atlantic

University. Retrieved January 14, 2000, from the World Wide Web: http://www.fau.edu/netiquette/netiquette.html.

Robb, T. N. (1995/1996). Web projects for the ESL/EFL class: Famous Japanese personages. *Computer Assisted English Language Learning, 6*(4), 21–24.

Robb, T. N. (1996). *E-mail keypals for language fluency* (Rev. ed). Retrieved May 30, 1999, from the World Wide Web: http://www.kyoto-su.ac.jp/~trobb /keypals.html. (Originally published in *Foreign Language Notes,* Vol. 38, No. 3, pp. 8–10)

Robb, T. N. (Ed.). (n.d.). *Famous personages in Japan.* Kyoto, Japan: Kyoto Sangyo University. Retrieved January 13, 2000, from the World Wide Web: http://www.kyoto-su.ac.jp/information/famous.

Rosen, D. J., with Macdonald, T., & Kamiya, A. (1999). *Virtual visits.* Boston: Metro Boston Community Wide Education and Information Service. Retrieved January 13, 2000, from the World Wide Web: http://www2 .wgbh.org/mbcweis/ltc/alri/vv.html.

Rosen, L. (1995). World news abroad. In M. Warschauer (Ed.), *Virtual connections: Online activities and projects for networking language learners* (pp. 268–271). Honolulu: University of Hawai'i, Second Language Teaching and Curriculum Center.

Rossetti, P. (1997). *Online English.* Vancouver, Canada: Vancouver English. Retrieved January 12, 2000, from the World Wide Web: http://www .geocities.com/Athens/Olympus/9260/online.html.

St. John, E., & Cash, D. (1995). Language learning via e-mail: Demonstrable success with German. In M. Warschauer (Ed.), *Virtual connections: Online activities and projects for networking language learners* (pp. 191–197). Honolulu: University of Hawai'i, Second Language Teaching and Curriculum Center.

Sandholtz, J. H., Ringstaff, C., & Dwyer, D. C. (1997). *Teaching with technology: Creating student-centered classrooms.* New York: Teachers College Press.

SARC online virus and hoax encyclopedia. (2000). Cupertino, CA: Symantec. Retrieved January 14, 2000, from the World Wide Web: http://www .symantec.com/avcenter/vinfodb.html.

Sayers, D. (1990, November). *Interscholastic exchanges in Celestin Freinet's Modern School Movement: Implications for computer-mediated student writing networks.* Paper presented at the North American Freinet Conference, St. Catharine's, Canada. (ERIC Document Reproduction Service No. ED 358 037)

Sayers, D. (1993). Distance team teaching and computer learning networks. *TESOL Journal, 3*(1), 19–23.

Schultz, J. (2000). Computers and collaborative writing in the foreign language curriculum. In M. Warschauer & R. Kern (Eds.), *Network-based language teaching: Concepts and practice* (pp. 121–150). Cambridge: Cambridge University Press.

Self-study quizzes for ESL students. (1999). Nagoya, Japan: Internet TESL Journal. Retrieved January 5, 2000, from the World Wide Web: http://www .aitech.ac.jp/~iteslj/quizzes/index.html.

Self-study quizzes for ESL students project. (1999). Nagoya, Japan: Internet TESL Journal. Retrieved January 5, 2000, from the World Wide Web: http://www .aitech.ac.jp/~iteslj/quizzes/project.html.

Shadian, R. (1997). QuizMaker 2.0 Demo [Computer software]. (Available from http://www.mrtc.org/~twright/quizzes/quizcenter/makerdemo.html)

Shetzer, H. (1997). *Critical reflection on the use of e-mail in teaching English as a second language.* Unpublished master's thesis, University of Illinois at Urbana-Champaign. Retrieved January 4, 2000, from the World Wide Web: http://www.newtierra.com/shetzer97.

Shetzer, H. (1999a). *How to create a basic Web page with HTML.* Retrieved January 4, 2000, from the World Wide Web: http://www.newtierra.com /tags.html.

Shetzer, H. (1999b). *How to create a basic Web page with Netscape Composer.* Retrieved January 12, 2000, from the World Wide Web: http://www .newtierra.com/composer.

Shetzer, H. (2000a). *English through Web page creation.* Retrieved February 22, 2000, from the World Wide Web: http://www.newtierra.com/ucsb.

Shetzer, H. (2000b). *How to use WS_FTP in the Storke Lab.* Retrieved February 22, 2000, from the World Wide Web: http://www.newtierra.com/ucsb /ftp.html.

Shetzer, H., & Warschauer, M. (2000). An electronic literacy approach to network-based language teaching. In M. Warschauer & R. Kern (Eds.), *Network-based language teaching: Concepts and practice* (pp. 171–185). Cambridge: Cambridge University Press.

Shneiderman, B. (1997). Foreword. In R. Debski, J. Gassin, & M. Smith (Eds.), *Language learning through social computing* (pp. v–viii). Melbourne: Applied Linguistics Association of Australia.

Shockwave Player [Computer software]. (1999). San Francisco: Macromedia. (Available from http://www.macromedia.com/shockwave/download)

SLART-L. (n.d.). Retrieved December 12, 1999, from the World Wide Web: http://listserv.cuny.edu/archives/slart-l.html.

Soh, B.-L., & Soon, Y. P. (1991). English by e-mail: Creating a global classroom via the medium of computer technology. *ELT Journal, 45,* 287–292.

Spath, J. (n.d.). *ISO country codes.* Retrieved January 5, 2000, from the World Wide Web: http://www.bcpl.net/~jspath/isocodes.html.

Sperling, D. (1999). *ESL Web guide.* Retrieved December 13, 1999, from the World Wide Web: http://eslcafe.com/search.

Sperling, D. (2000). *ESL discussion center.* Retrieved January 5, 2000, from the World Wide Web: http://eslcafe.com/discussion.

Stoller, F. (1997, October). Project work: A means to promote language content. *English Teaching Forum,* p. 2.

Sullivan, N., & Pratt, E. (1996). A comparative study of two ESL writing environments: A computer-assisted classroom and a traditional oral classroom. *System, 24,* 491–501.

Surviving in the one-computer classroom. (1999). East Brunswick, NJ: Educational Technology Training Center of Middlesex County. Retrieved January 12, 2000, from the World Wide Web: http://www.techtrain.org/curriculum/1computr.htm.

Tango for Filemaker Pro [Computer software]. (1997). Austin, TX: Pervasive Software. (Available from http://www.everyware.com)

Tantsetthi, T., Williams, G., & Reynolds, R. (n.d.). *English language teaching in Asia mailing list.* Retrieved December 10, 1999, from the World Wide Web: http://www.nectec.or.th/users/ttesol/eltasia.htm.

Teleport Pro [Computer software]. (1997). Cambridge, MA: Tennyson Maxwell. (Available from http://www.tenmax.com/teleport/pro)

Tella, S. (1992a). *Boys, girls and e-mail: A case study in Finnish senior secondary schools* (Research Report No. 110). Helsinki, Finland: University of Helsinki, Department of Teacher Education.

Tella, S. (1992b). *Talking shop via e-mail: A thematic and linguistic analysis of electronic mail communication* (Research Report No. 99). Helsinki, Finland: University of Helsinki, Department of Teacher Education.

Tella, S. (1996). Foreign languages and modern technology: Harmony or hell? In M. Warschauer (Ed.), *Telecollaboration in foreign language learning.* Honolulu: University of Hawai'i, Second Language Teaching and Curriculum Center.

Tenopir, C., & King, D. W. (1997). Trends in scientific scholarly journal publishing in the United States. *Journal of Scholarly Publishing, 28,* 135–170.

TESOL on-line workshops for ESOL professionals. (1999). Alexandria, VA: TESOL. Retrieved January 13, 2000, from the World Wide Web: http://www.tesol.org/edprg/1999/olw.html.

Thalman, L. (Ed.). (2000). *Online courses and methodology for learning and teaching English and French.* Paris: WebFrance International. Retrieved January 13, 2000, from the World Wide Web: http://www.wfi.fr/volterre/onlinecourses.html.

Tribble, C., & Jones, G. (1990). *Concordancing in the classroom.* Essex, England: Longman.

URL Manager Pro [Computer software]. (1999). Amsterdam: Alco Blom Software. (Available from http://www.url-manager.com)

Using the Internet in the one computer classroom. (1997). Portland, OR: David Douglas School District. Retrieved January 12, 2000, from the World Wide Web: http://millpark.ddouglas.k12.or.us/onecomp.html.

Vilmi, R. (1995). International environment activity. In M. Warschauer (Ed.), *Virtual connections: Online activities and projects for networking language learners* (pp. 205–207). Honolulu: University of Hawai'i, Second Language Teaching and Curriculum Center.

Vilmi, R. (1998). *King's road project.* Retrieved January 13, 2000, from the World Wide Web: http://www.hut.fi/~rvilmi/King.

Vilmi, R. (n.d.). *Environment activity.* Retrieved January 12, 2000, from the World Wide Web: http://www.hut.fi/~rvilmi/autumn94/environment.html.

Wang, Y. M. (1993). *E-mail dialogue journaling in an ESL reading and writing classroom.* Unpublished doctoral dissertation, University of Oregon at Eugene.

Warschauer, M. (1995a). *E-mail for English teaching.* Alexandria, VA: TESOL.

Warschauer, M. (Ed.). (1995b). *Virtual connections: Online activities and projects for networking language learners.* Honolulu: University of Hawai'i, Second Language Teaching and Curriculum Center.

Warschauer, M. (1996a). Comparing face-to-face and electronic communication in the second language classroom. *CALICO Journal, 13*(2), 7–26.

Warschauer, M. (1996b). Motivational aspects of using computers for writing and communication. In M. Warschauer (Ed.), *Telecollaboration in foreign language learning: Proceedings of the Hawai'i symposium* (pp. 29–46). Honolulu: University of Hawai'i, Second Language Teaching and Curriculum Center.

Warschauer, M. (1997). Computer-mediated collaborative learning: Theory and practice. *Modern Language Journal, 81,* 470–481.

Warschauer, M. (1998a). Online learning in sociocultural context. *Anthropology & Education Quarterly, 29,* 68–88.

Warschauer, M. (1998b). Technology and indigenous language revitalization: Analyzing the experience of Hawai'i. *Canadian Modern Language Review, 55,* 140–161.

Warschauer, M. (1999). *Electronic literacies: Language, culture, and power in online education.* Mahwah, NJ: Erlbaum.

Warschauer, M. (n.d.). *Papyrus news.* Retrieved December 13, 1999, from the World Wide Web: http://www.lll.hawaii.edu/web/faculty/markw/papyrus-news.html.

WebBBS [Computer software]. (1999). Omaha, NE: Affordable Web Space Design. (Available from http://awsd.com/scripts/webbbs)

WebCT [Computer software]. (1999). Vancouver, Canada: WebCT Educational Technologies. (Available from http://209.87.17.102/webct)

WebFX [Computer software]. (1999). Davis, CA: New Breed Software. (Available from http://www.newbreedsoftware.com/webfx)

WebWhacker [Computer software]. (1999). Draper, UT: Blue Squirrrel. (Available from http://www.bluesquirrel.com/products/whacker/whacker.html)

White, A. (1998). *Internet scavenger hunts.* Retrieved January 13, 2000, from the World Wide Web: http://home.earthlink.net/~athearn.

Williams, R., & Tollett, J. (1998). *The non-designer's Web book.* Berkeley, CA: Peachpit Press.

Wilson, E. (1994, April). *On-line electronic libraries.* Paper presented at the Ninth British and Irish Legal Education Technology Association Conference, Coventry, England. Retrieved May 30, 1999 from the World Wide Web: http://www.bileta.ac.uk/94papers/ewilson.html.

Windows Media Technologies 4.1 [Computer software]. (1999). Redmond, WA: Microsoft. (Available from http://www.microsoft.com/windows/windowsmedia)

Wolfe-Quintero, K., Inagaki, S., & Kim, H.-Y. (1998). *Second language development in writing: Measures of fluency, accuracy & complexity.* Honolulu: University of Hawai'i Press.

WordPerfect (Version 6.1) [Computer software]. (1997). Ottawa, Canada: Corel.

WWWebster dictionary. (2000). Springfield, MA: Merriam-Webster. Retrieved January 14, 2000, from the World Wide Web: http://www.m-w.com/netdict.htm.

Yates, S. J. (1996). Oral and written linguistic aspects of computer conferencing: A corpus-based study. In S. C. Herring (Ed.), *Computer-mediated communication: Linguistic, social and cross-cultural perspectives* (pp. 29–46). Amsterdam: Benjamins.

Zuboff, S. (1988). *In the age of the smart machine: The future of work and power.* New York: Basic Books.

Appendix A:
Index of
Internet Addresses

Adobe Acrobat Reader: http://www.adobe.com/products/acrobat/readstep.html
Adobe GoLive: http://www.adobe.com/products/golive/main.html
Adobe PageMill: http://www.adobe.com/products/pagemill/main.html
Adobe Photoshop (Adobe ImageReady): http://www.adobe.com/products/photoshop/main.html
Adult ESL Homeownership Education: http://www.cal.org/public/fannie.htm
Advanced English Composition Online for International Students: http://vms.cc.wmich.edu/~kubota/englishonline99.htm
Alliance for Computers and Writing: http://english.ttu.edu/acw
All-in-One Search Page: http://www.allonesearch.com
AltaVista: http://www.altavista.com
Amazon.com: http://www.amazon.com
American Association for Applied Linguistics (AAAL): http://www.aaal.org
American Council on the Teaching of Foreign Languages (ACTFL): http://www.actfl.org
American Language Review: http://www.alr.org
Animation Factory: http://www.animfactory.com
Anvil Studio: http://www.AnvilStudio.com
AOL Instant Messenger: http://www.aol.com/aim
APA Writing Style Guide: http://www.ldl.net/~bill/apatwo.htm
AskERIC: http://ericir.syr.edu
Aspera PrivaTeacher: http://www.PrivaTeacher.com

Background Gallery: http://www.geocities.com/SoHo/Gallery/6467
Barnesandnoble.com: http://www.barnesandnoble.com
BBC Schools Online: http://www.bbc.co.uk/education/schools
Berkeley Digital Library SunSITE: http://sunsite.berkeley.edu
Blackboard: http://www.blackboard.com
British Broadcasting Corp. (BBC): http://www.bbc.co.uk

CALL-EJ Online: http://www.lerc.ritsumei.ac.jp/callej
CELIA at La Trobe University: http://www.latrobe.edu.au/www/education
   /celia/celia.html
Center for Applied Linguistics (CAL): http://www.cal.org
CGI Collection, The: http://www.itm.com/cgicollection
CGIemail Home Page, The: http://Web.mit.edu/wwwdev/cgiemail
Child Language Data Exchange System (CHILDES): http://
   childes.psy.cmu.edu
Christian Science Monitor, The: http://www.csmonitor.com
Cities Project: http://www.nyu.edu/pages/hess/cities.html
ClipArtDownload.com: http://www.clipartdownload.com
Clip Art for Web Sites: http://www.graphicmaps.com/clipart.htm
CNET Builder.com: http://builder.cnet.com
CNN.com: http://www.cnn.com
Coast to Coast Project: http://gwis2.circ.gwu.edu/~gwvcusas/coasttocoast.htm
Colleges and Universities: http://www.hoyle.com/distance/college.html
Collins CobuildDirect: http://titania.cobuild.collins.co.uk/direct_info.html
Collins Cobuild Student Dictionary Online: http://springbank.linguistics.ruhr-
   uni-bochum.de/ccsd
CommonSpace: http://www.sixthfloor.com/CS1.html
Computer-Assisted Language Instruction Consortium (CALICO):
   http://www.calico.org
Computer Economics: http://www.computereconomics.com
"Computer-Mediated Collaborative Learning: Theory and Practice":
   http://www.lll.hawaii.edu/web/faculty/markw/cmcl.html
*Computer-Mediated Communication in Foreign Language Education: An
   Annotated Bibliography*: http://www.lll.hawaii.edu/nflrc/NetWorks/NW3
Confer V: http://www.wmich.edu/docs/3803.html
CONTENT-ESL: http://members.aol.com/Drlfk/Content-ESL.html
Copyright Circulars: http://lcWeb2.loc.gov/ammem/copcirc.html
Copyright Website, The: http://www.benedict.com
*Critical Reflection on the Use of E-Mail in Teaching English as a Second
   Language*: http://www.newtierra.com/shetzer97
Culture Web Site Project: http://www.esl-lab.com/courses/project.html

CU-SeeME: http://www.wpine.com/Products/CU-SeeMe
Cutting Edge CALL Demos: http://www-writing.berkeley.edu/chorus/call
/cuttingedge.html

Daedalus Integrated Writing Environment (Daedalus InterChange):
http://www.daedalus.com
Daily Brief: http://www.incinc.net
"Daily Double Download": http://www.zdnet.com/yil/content/depts/doubled
/dlcurrent/dlcurrent.html
Dave's ESL Cafe: http://eslcafe.com
Delphi Forums: http://www.delphi.com
Digital Diploma Mills: http://communication.ucsd.edu/dl
Digital Libraries Initiative: http://www.dli2.nsf.gov
Director: http://www.macromedia.com/software/director
Directory of Online Colleges, Internet Universities, and Training Institutes:
http://www.geteducated.com/dlsites.htm
Distance Education Online Symposium (DEOS) (1999): http://
www.ed.psu.edu/acsde/DEOS.html
Distance Learning: Promise or Threat?: http://www.rohan.sdsu.edu/faculty
/feenberg/TELE3.HTM
Dogpile: http://dogpile.com
Domain Name Registries Around the World: http://www.uninett.no/navn
/domreg.html
Download.com: http://www.download.com
Dr. Solomon's Software: http://www.drsolomon.com
Dreamweaver: http://www.macromedia.com/software/dreamweaver

East Boston Harborside Goes to a Computer Store!: http://www2.wgbh.org
/mbcweis/esquare/virtualfront.htm
Ed Tech Tools: Free On-Line Services for Educators: http://motted.hawaii.edu
Edupage: http://www.educause.edu/pub/edupage/edupage.html
eGroups.com: http://www.egroups.com
Electric Library: http://www.elibrary.com
*Electronic Reference Formats Recommended by the American Psychological
Association*: http://www.apa.org/journals/webref.html
ELTASIA-L: http://www.nectec.or.th/users/ttesol/eltasia.htm
ELT Journal: http://www3.oup.co.uk/eltj
ELT Spectrum: http://www1.oup.co.uk/cite/oup/elt/magazine/magazine.html
E-Mail Keypals for Language Fluency: http://www.kyoto-su.ac.jp/~trobb
/keypals.html

E-Mail, the Web, and MOOs: Developing the Writing Skills of University Students in Cyberspace: http://gwis.circ.gwu.edu/~washweb /proceedings.html

E-Mail Tops Telephone, Say HR Execs: http://www.amanet.org/survey /hrc98.htm

"eMarketer Tallies the Number of E-Mail Messages Sent in 1999": http://www.emarketer.com/estats/020199_email.html

Endangered Animals of India: http://cyberfair.gsn.org/falcon/narrative.html

English for Internet: http://www.study.com

English for Writing Up Research: http://www.dundee.ac.uk/languagestudies /esp2.htm#research

English Listening Lounge: http://www.englishlistening.com

English Spark Online Magazine: http://humanum.arts.cuhk.edu.hk/~cmc /engspark

English Teaching Forum Online: http://e.usia.gov/forum

English Through Web Page Creation: http://www.newtierra.com/ucsb

Englishtown: http://englishtown.com

Environment Activity: http://www.hut.fi/~rvilmi/autumn94/environment.html

Environmental Change Documentary: http://www.miyazaki-mic.ac.jp/classes /fall98/aisenv/projects/project1.html

E-Pals: http://www.britcoun.org.hk/epals/epals_new.html

ERIC: http://www.accesseric.org

ERIC Clearinghouse on Languages and Linguistics: http://www.cal.org/ericcll

ESL Discussion Center: http://eslcafe.com/discussion

ESL Magazine: http://www.eslmag.com

ESLoop: http://www.tesol.net/esloop

ESL Study Hall, The: http://gwis2.circ.gwu.edu/~gwvcusas

ESL Web Guide: http://eslcafe.com/search

Everychat: http://www.everysoft.com/everychat

Extensible Markup Language (XML): http://www.w3.org/XML

Famous Personages in Japan: http://www.kyoto-su.ac.jp/information/famous

Fireworks: http://www.macromedia.com/software/fireworks

FLTEACH: http://www.cortland.edu/flteach

Forum One Index: http://www.forumone.com

Franklin Institute Science Museum: http://sln.fi.edu

Free Graphics Resources: http://www.thefreesite.com/freegraphics.htm

Freedback.com: http://www.freedback.com

Free Webpage Provider Review, The: http://fwpreview.ngworld.net

German Culture Pages in English: http://www.geocities.com/Athens/Forum /8383

GifOptimizer: http://www.gifoptimizer.com

GIFSplit: http://www.jbarchuk.com/gifsplit

Google: http://www.google.com

"Google: We're Down With ODP": http://www.salon.com/tech/feature /2000/03/24/google_odp/index.html

Gossamer Threads: http://www.gossamer-threads.com

Grammar Safari: http://deil.lang.uiuc.edu/web.pages/grammarsafari.html

GraphicConverter: http://www.lemkesoft.de

"The Guidelines Net Project": http://www.vcu.edu/cspweb/gnp_caell.html

Hello: http://www.hello.com.tw

HiNetCity: http://netcity.web.hinet.net

Homebuying for Everyone: http://www2.wgbh.org/mbcweis/ltc/final /vvhome.html

Home Page: http://www.claris.com/products/hp_home.html

HotBot: http://hotbot.lycos.com

Hotmail: http://www.hotmail.com

Hot Potatoes: http://Web.uvic.ca/hrd/halfbaked

"How Many Online?": http://www.nua.ie/surveys/how_many_online /index.html

How to Create a Basic Web Page With HTML: http://www.newtierra.com /tags.html

How to Create a Basic Web Page With Netscape Composer: http://www .newtierra.com/composer

"How to Make a Successful ESL/EFL Teacher's Web Page": http://www.aitech.ac.jp/~iteslj/Articles/Kelly-MakePage

How to Use WS_FTP in the Storke Lab: http://www.newtierra.com/ucsb /ftp.html

HTML: An Interactive Tutorial for Beginners: http://www.davesite.com /webstation/html

HTML Goodies: http://www.htmlgoodies.com

HTML Home Page: http://www.w3.org/MarkUp

IconBAZAAR: http://www.iconbazaar.com

ICQ: http://www.icq.com

Ideas for the One Computer Classroom: http://danenet.wicip.org/mmsd-it/tlc /1comprm.html

Inspiration: http://www.inspiration.com

Interactive Listening Comprehension Practice: http://deil.lang.uiuc.edu/lcra

International Association of Teachers of English as a Foreign Language (IATEFL): http://www.iatefl.org

International House Net Languages: http://www.netlanguages.com

International Language Testing Association: http://www.surrey.ac.uk/ELI/ilta/ilta.html

International Protection of Copyright and Neighboring Rights: http://www.ompi.org/eng/general/copyrght/intro.htm

International Review of Applied Linguistics in Language Teaching: http://www3.oup.co.uk/iral

Internet Classroom Assistant: http://www.nicenet.org

Internet Corporation for Assigned Names and Numbers (ICANN): http://www.icann.org

"The Internet in the Classroom": http://www.eslmag.com/Article.html

Internet Movie Database: http://www.imdb.com

Internet Scavenger Hunts: http://home.earthlink.net/~athearn

Internet TESL Journal, The: http://www.aitech.ac.jp/~iteslj

ISO Country Codes: http://www.bcpl.net/~jspath/isocodes.html

Jack's English Classroom: http://NetCity1.web.hinet.net/UserData/tseng913

Japan Association for Language Teaching (JALT): http://www.jalt.org

Japanese Food Recipe Page: http://www.kyoto-su.ac.jp/information/recipes

JPEG Wizard: http://www.jpegwizard.com

Kairos: http://english.ttu.edu/kairos

Karin's ESL PartyLand: http://www.eslpartyland.com

Kenji Kitao's Home Page: http://202.23.150.181/users/kkitao

Keypal Opportunities for Students: http://ilc2.doshisha.ac.jp/users/kkitao/online/www/keypal.htm

KeyPals Club: http://www.mightymedia.com/keypals

King's Road Project: http://www.hut.fi/~rvilmi/King

Kyoto Restaurant Project: http://www.kyoto-su.ac.jp/information/restaurant

Language Learning & Technology: http://polyglot.cal.msu.edu/llt

Language Teacher Online, The: http://langue.hyper.chubu.ac.jp/jalt/pub/tlt

Learning Resources: http://literacynet.org/cnnsf

LIBCAT: A Guide to Library Resources on the Internet: http://www.metronet.lib.mn.us/lc/lc1.cfm

Libweb: http://sunsite.berkeley.edu/Libweb

LINGUIST: http://www.linguistlist.org

Linguistic Funland: http://www.linguistic-funland.com

Linguistic Society of America (LSA): http://www.lsadc.org

Linkman: http://www.outertech.com
Links 2.0: http://www.gossamer-threads.com/scripts/links
Liszt, the Mailing List Directory: http://www.liszt.com
Literature Online: http://lion.chadwyck.com
LLTI-L: http://iall.net/LLTI.html
Longman ELT Connection: http://www.awl-elt.com
Louvre: http://www.louvre.fr
LTEST-L: http://www.surrey.ac.uk/ELI/ltest-l.html
Lview Pro: http://www.lview.com
Lycos: http://www.lycos.com

Matt's Script Archive: http://worldwidemart.com/scripts
McAfee: http://www.mcafee.com
MediaBuilder: Animation Factory: http://www.animfactory.com
Microsoft FrontPage: http://www.microsoft.com/frontpage
Microsoft Internet Explorer: http://www.microsoft.com/windows/IE
Microsoft NetMeeting: http://www.microsoft.com/netmeeting
Microsoft WebTV: http://www.webtv.com
Microsoft Word: http://www.microsoft.com/office/word
"MIDI for the Masses": http://www.wdvl.com/Multimedia/Sound/Audio
    /midi.html
MLA Style: http://www.mla.org/main_stl.htm
Modern Language Journal, The: http://polyglot.lss.wisc.edu/mlj

NAFSA: Association of International Educators: http://www.nafsa.org
National Clearinghouse for Bilingual Education (NCBE): http://
    www.ncbe.gwu.edu
National Council of Teachers of English (NCTE): http://www.ncte.org
National Foreign Language Resource Center (NFLRC): http://
    www.lll.hawaii.edu/nflrc
National Gallery of Art: http://www.nga.gov
NETEACH-L: http://www.ilc.cuhk.edu.hk/english/neteach/main.html
Netiquette Home Page: http://www.fau.edu/netiquette/netiquette.html
NetLearn Languages: http://www.nll.co.uk
NetObjects Fusion: http://www.netobjects.com
Netscape Browser Plug-Ins: http://www.netscape.com/plugins
Netscape Communicator (Netscape Composer): http://home.netscape.com
    /computing/download
Netscape Netcenter: http://www.netscape.com
Netscape Search: http://search.netscape.com
Network Solutions: http://www.networksolutions.com

Newbury House Online Dictionary: http://nhd.heinle.com

NewDeal Inc.: http://www.newdealinc.com

NEW-LIST: http://scout.cs.wisc.edu/scout/caservices/new-list

Newport Pacific University: http://www.asiapacificu.edu

NewPromise.Com: Online Education Directory: http://www.newpromise.com

NewsLibrary: http://www.newslibrary.com

Newspapers Online: http://www.newspapers.com

Newsweek: http://www.newsweek.com

New Tierra: Distance Learning: http://www.newtierra.com/links
/DistanceLearning

New Tierra Links: http://www.newtierra.com/links

New York Times: http://www.nytimes.com

New York Times Learning Network, The: http://www.nytimes.com/learning

Northern Light: http://northernlight.com

O-Hayo Sensei: http://www.ohayosensei.com

One Computer Classroom, The: http://www.remc11.k12.mi.us/bcisd/classres
/onecomp.htm

Online Courses and Methodology for Learning and Teaching English and French:
http://www.wfi.fr/volterre/onlinecourses.html

On-Line Electronic Libraries: http://www.bileta.ac.uk/94papers/ewilson.html

Online English: http://www.geocities.com/Athens/Olympus/9260/online.html

Online ESL Courses (Tower of English): http://members.tripod.com
/~towerofenglish/onlinecourses.htm

Online Writing Lab: http://owl.english.purdue.edu

Open Directory Project: http://dmoz.org

Open Learning International: http://olionline.com

Oxford University Press: http://www.oup.co.uk

Paint Shop Pro: http://www.jasc.com/psp6dl.html

Papyrus News: http://www.lll.hawaii.edu/web/faculty/markw/papyrus-
news.html

Plagiarism.org: http://plagiarism.org

"Processes and Outcomes in Networked Classroom Interaction: Defining the
Research Agenda for L2 Computer-Assisted Classroom Discussion":
http://polyglot.cal.msu.edu/llt/vol1num1

Project Gutenberg: http://www.gutenberg.net

Publication Manual of the American Psychological Association: http://
www.apa.org/books/pubman.html

QuickTime 4 Pro: http://www.apple.com/quicktime/authoring
QuickTime VR Authoring: http://www.apple.com/quicktime/qtvr
QuizMaker 2.0 Demo: http://www.mrtc.org/~twright/quizzes/quizcenter
  /makerdemo.html

Randall's ESL Cyber Listening Lab: http://www.esl-lab.com
RealPlayer: http://www.real.com
RealProducer Plus: http://www.realnetworks.com/products/producerplus
Red Rock Eater News Service: http://dlis.gseis.ucla.edu/people/pagre/rre.html
Remote Technical Assistance: http://escher.cs.ucdavis.edu:1024
Research-It!: http://www.itools.com/research-it
Resources for Moderators and Facilitators of Online Discussions: http://
  www.emoderators.com/moderators.shtml

SARC Online Virus and Hoax Encyclopedia: http://www.symantec.com
  /avcenter/vinfodb.html
schMOOze University: http://schmooze.hunter.cuny.edu:8888
Scripts for Educators: http://www.linguistic-funland.com/scripts
Scripts Home, The: http://www.virtualcenter.com/scripts2
Self-Study Quizzes for ESL Students: http://www.aitech.ac.jp/~iteslj/quizzes
  /index.html
Self-Study Quizzes for ESL Students Project: http://www.aitech.ac.jp/~iteslj
  /quizzes/project.html
Shareware.com: http://shareware.cnet.com
Shockwave Player: http://www.macromedia.com/shockwave/download
Sites Neteachers Thought Were Cool!: http://www.linguistic-funland.com
  /neteach.html
SLART-L: http://listserv.cuny.edu/archives/slart-l.html
SL-Lists: http://www.latrobe.edu.au/www/education/sl/sl.html
SmartPlanet.com: http://www.smartplanet.com
SoundRecorder: http://dgrwww.epfl.ch/~jenny
Speakeasy Studio and Café: http://morrison.wsu.edu/studio
Spirit of Christmas, The: http://www.malhatlantica.pt/teresadeca
  /spiritofxmas.htm
Strategies and Applications for the One Computer Classroom: http://
  www.lburkhart.com/elem/strat.htm
Surviving in the One-Computer Classroom: http://www.techtrain.org
  /curriculum/1computr.htm
Sydney Morning Herald, The: http://www.smh.com.au
Symantec Corp.: http://www.symantec.com

Talk City: http://www.talkcity.com

Tango for Filemaker Pro: http://www.everyware.com

Teaching in the Community Colleges Online Conference: http://leahi.kcc.hawaii.edu/tcc2000

TEFL China Tea House: http://teflchina.com

TeleCampus: http://apsis.telecampus.edu

Teleport Pro: http://www.tenmax.com/teleport/pro

TESLCA-L: http://www.ling.lancs.ac.uk/staff/visitors/kenji/lis-tesl.htm

TESL-EJ: http://www.kyoto-su.ac.jp/information/tesl-ej

TESOL: http://www.tesol.org

TESOL Matters: http://www.tesol.org/pubs/articles/tm9912.html

TESOL On-Line Workshops for ESOL Professionals: http://www.tesol.org/edprg/1999/olw.html

TESOL Quarterly: http://www.tesol.org/pubs/magz/tq.html

ThinkQuest: http://www.thinkquest.org

3D Webscapes: http://www.sonic.net/~lberlin/new/3dnscape.html

Tile.Net: http://tile.net

Time: http://www.time.com

Times, The: http://www.the-times.co.uk

Totally Free Stuff: http://www.totallyfreestuff.com

Tower of English: http://members.tripod.com/~towerofenglish

Tripod: http://www.tripod.lycos.com

Tucows Network: http://www.tucows.com

Uffizi Gallery: http://www.uffizi.firenze.it

Ultra Recorder: http://members.aol.com/ejc3/Ultra.html

UnCoverWeb: http://uncweb.carl.org

University of Surrey: http://www.surrey.ac.uk

University of Wisconsin, Madison, Distance Education Certificate Program: http://uwex.edu/disted/depd/certpro.html

URL Manager Pro: http://www.url-manager.com

US-SiberLink: http://www.gwu.edu/~washweb/us-siberlink.htm

"US-SiberLink Internet Project": http://ccnic14.kyoto-su.ac.jp/information/tesl-ej/ej15/a1.html

Using the Internet in the One Computer Classroom: http://millpark.ddouglas.k12.or.us/onecomp.html

Using TESL-L for Research and Teaching English: http://www.ling.lancs.ac.uk/staff/visitors/kenji/lis-tesl.htm

Virtual High School: http://vhs.concord.org

Virtual School Visit, A: http://www.otan.dni.us/webfarm/emailproject
/school.htm

Virtual University: http://www.vu.org

Virtual Visits: http://www2.wgbh.org/mbcweis/ltc/alri/vv.html

Vocabulary University: http://www.vocabulary.com

Wall Street Journal, The: http://www.wsj.com

"Wandering the Web": http://www.tesol.org/pubs/magz/wanweb.html

Washington Post, The: http://www.washingtonpost.com

WebBBS: http://awsd.com/scripts/Webbbs

Web Clip Art: http://Webclipart.miningco.com

WebCT: http://209.87.17.102/webct

Web Developer.com: http://www.Webdeveloper.com

Web Developer's Journal: http://Webdevelopersjournal.com

Web Developer's Virtual Library: http://www.wdvl.com

Webfolios: http://www.maltar.org.il/k12/arazim/eng/portfols.htm

WebFX: http://www.newbreedsoftware.com/webfx

Webmaster's Guild, The: http://www.thedaily.washington.edu/staff/martin
/Webmasters.guild

Webmonkey: The Web Developer's Resource: http://www.hotwired.lycos.com
/webmonkey

Web of On-Line Dictionaries, A: http://www.facstaff.bucknell.edu/rbeard
/diction.html

Webopedia: http://webopaedia.com

WebReference.com: http://www.Webreference.com

WebScripts: http://awsd.com/scripts

Web Scripts: Examples for Language Learning: http://www.fln.vcu.edu/cgi
/archive.html

Web66: A K12 World Wide Web Project: http://web66.coled.umn.edu

WebWhacker: http://www.bluesquirrel.com/products/whacker/whacker.html

What's the Internet?: http://www.esl-lab.com/courses/start.html

Windows Media Technologies: http://www.microsoft.com/windows
/windowsmedia

Windy's Design Studio: http://www.windyWeb.com

World Intellectual Property Organization: http://www.wipo.org

World Lecture Hall: http://www.utexas.edu/world/lecture

World Wide Arts Resources: http://wwar.com

World Wide Web Consortium, The: http://www.w3.org

World Wide Web Scavenger Hunt: http://www.crpc.rice.edu/CRPC/GT/
sboone/Lessons/Titles/hunt/hunt.html

WOW! Washington on the Web: http://gwis2.circ.gwu.edu/~gwvcusas
/WOWHOME.htm
Writing Around the World—Telecommunications and English: The Cities Project:
http://www.nyu.edu/pages/hess/cities.html
WWWebster Dictionary: http://www.m-w.com/netdict.htm

XOOM.com: http://xoom.com

Yahoo!: http://www.yahoo.com
Yahoo! Education: Distance Learning: http://dir.yahoo.com/Education
/Distance_Learning
Yahoo! Education: Distance Learning: K–12: http://dir.yahoo.com/Education
/Distance_Learning/K_12
Yahoo! GeoCities: http://geocities.yahoo.com
Yahoo! Mail: http://mail.yahoo.com

ZyGraphics: http://www.zyris.com

Appendix B: Books for Further Reading

This appendix lists books that are useful for learning more about incorporating computers and the Internet in English language teaching.

Boswood, T. (1997). *New ways of using computers in language teaching.* Alexandria, VA: TESOL.

Chard, S. C. (1998). *The project approach book (one and two): Making curriculum come alive.* New York: Scholastic Press.

Cummins, J., & Sayers, D. (1997). *Brave new schools: Challenging cultural illiteracy through global learning networks.* New York: St. Martin's Press.

Debski, R., Gassin, J., & Smith, M. (Eds.). (1997). *Language learning through social computing.* Melbourne: Applied Linguistics Association of Australia.

Egbert, J., & Hanson-Smith, E. (Eds.). (1999). *CALL environments: Research, practice, and critical issues.* Alexandria, VA: TESOL.

Fried-Booth, D. (1996). *Project work.* New York: Oxford University Press.

Healey, D., & Johnson, N. (Eds.). (1999). *1999 TESOL CALL Interest Section software list.* Alexandria, VA: TESOL.

Heide, A., & Stilborne, L. (1999). *The teacher's complete and easy guide to the Internet* (2nd ed.). New York: Teacher's College Press.

Katz, L. G., & Chard, S. C. (1995). *Engaging children's minds: The project approach.* Norwood, NJ: Ablex.

Sandholtz, J. H., Ringstaff, C., & Dwyer, D. C. (1997). *Teaching with technology: Creating student-centered classrooms.* New York: Teachers College Press.

Sharan, Y., & Sharan, S. (1992). *Expanding cooperative learning through group investigation.* New York: Teachers College Press.

Shelly, G. B., Cashman, T. J., & Repede, J. F. (1998). *Netscape Composer—creating Web pages.* Cambridge: Course Technology.

Sperling, D. (1997). *The Internet guide for English language teachers.* Upper Saddle River, NJ: Prentice Hall Regents.

Sperling, D. (1999). *Dave Sperling's Internet activity book.* Upper Saddle River, NJ: Prentice Hall Regents.

Taylor, K. (1999). *Introducing the Internet: A beginner's guide to the Internet.* Rowley, MA: Didax Educational Resources.

Warschauer, M. (1995). *E-mail for English teaching: Bringing the Internet and computer learning networks into the language classroom.* Alexandria, VA: TESOL.

Warschauer, M. (1996a). *Telecollaboration in foreign language learning.* Honolulu: University of Hawai'i Press.

Warschauer, M. (Ed.). (1996b). *Virtual connections: Online activities and projects for networking language learners.* Honolulu: University of Hawai'i Press.

Warschauer, M. (1999). *Electronic literacies: Language, culture, and power in online education.* Mahwah, NJ: Erlbaum.

Warschauer, M., & Kern, R. (Eds.). (2000). *Network-based language teaching: Concepts and practice.* New York: Cambridge University Press.

Wenden, A. (1998). *Learner strategies for learner autonomy.* New York: Prentice Hall.

Appendix C:
Journals for
Further Reading

This appendix lists the Web sites of professional journals related to language teaching and/or technology in education. Journals listed with an asterisk (*) make available for free the complete contents of current and back issues on their Web sites. The other journals listed provide a variety of information on their sites, ranging from subscription information to the contents of selected features or articles from past issues.

Computers and Language Teaching

CALL-EJ Online: http://www.lerc.ritsumei.ac.jp/callej
Computer Assisted Language Learning: http://www.swets.nl/sps/journals
     /call.html
Language Learning & Technology: http://polyglot.cal.msu.edu/llt
ReCALL Journal: http://www.hull.ac.uk/cti/eurocall/recall.htm
System: http://www.elsevier.nl/inca/publications/store/3/3/5

Computers and Writing/Communication

Computers and Composition: http://www.cwrl.utexas.edu/~ccjrn
Journal of Computer-Mediated Communication: http://www.ascusc.org/jcmc
Kairos: A Journal for Teachers of Writing in Webbed Environments:
     http://english.ttu.edu/kairos

Computers in Education

From Now On: The Educational Technology Journal: http://www.fno.org
TechKnowLogia: http://www.techKnowLogia.org
T.H.E. Journal Online: http://www.thejournal.com

English Language Teaching

ELT Journal: http://www3.oup.co.uk/eltj
ELT News & Views: http://www.eltnewsandviews.com
English Teaching Forum Online: http://e.usia.gov/forum
ESL Magazine: http://www.eslmag.com
The Internet TESL Journal: http://www.aitech.ac.jp/~iteslj
TESL-EJ: http://www.kyoto-su.ac.jp/information/tesl-ej
TESOL Journal: http://www.tesol.edu/pubs/magz/tj.html
TESOL Quarterly: http://www.tesol.edu/pubs/magz/tq.html

Appendix D: Glossary

absolute link: hyperlink that connects to a specific Internet address, such as http://www.nytimes.com. See *relative link*.

anonymous File Transfer Protocol (FTP): a system for sending files to or receiving files from a remote computer that is available to the public, without any special userid required.

AOL: America Online, a popular Internet service provider and on-line service.

ASCII: American Standard Code for Information Interchange; pure text without formatting or graphics.

asynchronous: not instantaneous. Asynchronous messages take anywhere from several seconds to several minutes (or sometimes several hours) to arrive and can be read at any time; the recipient need not be logged on at the time of delivery.

attachment: file that is appended to an e-mail message for delivery over the Internet.

bandwidth: amount of data that is transmitted across a set period of time.

baud: when data are being transmitting, the number of times the medium's state changes per second. For example, a 56,000-baud modem changes the signal it sends over the telephone line 56,000 times per second.

baud rate: the speed of a modem. A 56,000-baud modem is twice as fast as a 28,000-baud modem. See *baud* and *bps*.

BBS: See *bulletin board system*.

bcc: blind carbon copy (or blind courtesy copy); a copy of a message sent to someone without the primary addressee being notified.

binary file: file that includes, in addition to text, some kind of formatting, such as graphics, special code, sounds, photos, or video.

bit: smallest unit of information on a computer.

body: main part of an e-mail message, where the message is written (distinguished from the *header*).

bookmark: address of a Web page that you have saved for easy future access using a Web browser, such as Netscape Navigator; also used as a verb, meaning to save the address of a Web page into a bookmark file. In Microsoft Internet Explorer, bookmarks are referred to as *Favorites*.

bps: bits per second; the speed at which bits are transmitted over a communications medium; used synonymously with *baud rate* to refer to the speed of a modem.

browser: software used for looking at and accessing information on the World Wide Web. Popular browsers include Netscape Navigator and Microsoft Internet Explorer.

BTW: by the way, a common abbreviation used in e-mail.

bulletin board system (BBS): system that allows for the posting and reading of messages on a local network; sometimes also connected to the Internet.

button rollover: button or graphic link on a Web page that changes its appearance, usually by swapping images, when the mouse is positioned on top of it.

byte: 8 bits.

cache: location in a computer's memory where recently accessed material is stored. Recently visited Web sites can be maintained in the cache for fast access.

case sensitive: making a distinction between uppercase and lowercase letters. Internet addresses (URLs) are case sensitive. That is, if a URL that contains only lowercase letters (e.g., http://www.xxx.com) is typed with some uppercase letters (e.g., http://www.XXX.com), you will not reach the desired site.

cc: carbon copy (or courtesy copy).

CELIA: *Computer-Enhanced Language Instruction Archive*; an archive of computer-assisted language learning software accessible by Gopher and by anonymous FTP.

CGI script: See *common gateway interface script*.

chat room: area on a Web site that enables synchronous discussion.

click: verb that represents the action of pressing down on a mouse button, usually the sole button on a mouse connected to a Macintosh computer and the left button on a mouse connected to a computer running Microsoft Windows.

client: software that extracts some service from a server somewhere on the network on your behalf. For example, TinyFugue is a client that provides a special interface for working with MOO servers.

CMC: See *computer-mediated communication.*

common gateway interface (CGI) script: program or sequence of instructions that is written in a programming language (such as Perl) to exchange data between a Web browser and a Web server. Fill-in forms, for example, use CGI scripts to process information entered by users.

compression: act of making files smaller in size, as with file compression software such as WinZip.

computer-mediated communication (CMC): use of one or more computers to mediate or facilitate communication between two or more people.

cookie: message that stores information on your computer for later retrieval by a Web server. For example, if you register at a password-protected Web site, you can elect to save the password on your computer as a cookie for later retrieval and use by the Web site. You can set your browser to refuse cookies so as to maintain more privacy, but doing so might prevent you from making full use of some Web sites.

country code: abbreviation that represents the name of a country in an e-mail or Internet address (e.g., *jp* for Japan).

cyberspace: amorphous term used to refer to the world of electronic communication.

cybersurfing: using various tools to search for information on the Internet; also referred to as *surfing the Net.*

Daedalus InterChange: software for real-time communication in the composition and language classroom; a component of the software suite Daedalus Integrated Writing Environment.

database: electronic system that organizes information into different fields, records, and files that can be viewed, sorted, and organized.

digitize: convert into a digital form (i.e., a form stored in bits). For example, a video can be digitized and then edited on a computer, inserted in a Web document, or sent by e-mail.

directory: organizational structure on a computer running DOS or Microsoft Windows that may contain files. See *folder.*

discussion board: program on a Web site that enables you to have asynchronous conversations with others; also known as a *Web board.* The conversations are organized by subject heading, or thread.

diskette: storage mechanism for electronic information, usually with a capacity of either 1.4 or 2.5 megabytes.

domain: second part of an e-mail address, following the @ sign (e.g., *whitehouse.gov* in president@whitehouse.gov), indicating the particular computer that is hooked up to the Internet.

double-click: the act of clicking two times on the mouse button.

download: copy computer files in a direction closer to you (e.g., from a remote computer to your Internet directory or from your Internet directory to your personal computer).

e-commerce: See *electronic commerce.*

electronic commerce: business conducted on the Internet.

e-mail: electronic mail; a way of sending messages asynchronously between two or more individuals connected via computer; sometimes spelled *email.*

emoticon: symbol used to convey emotion in an e-mail message (e.g., :-) [a smile] or :-([a frown]); also referred to as a *smiley.*

Eudora: popular software for sending, receiving, and managing e-mail.

Extensible Markup Language (XML): coding language that describes the content of a Web page, such as the pictures or text contained in the page, in contrast to *HTML,* which describes the physical appearance of the page.

extension: letters at the end of file names that designate the file type. Common extensions include *.doc* for document, *.txt* for ASCII text file, and *.html* for hypertext document.

external link: link that connects to a resource stored not on the local computer but on a remote computer.

FAQ: (a) frequently asked question; (b) more commonly, a list of frequently asked questions pertaining to the use of a particular Usenet newsgroup or e-mail discussion list.

Favorites: addresses of Web pages that are saved for easy future reference using the Web browser Microsoft Internet Explorer; referred to as *bookmarks* in many other Web browsers.

file name: name assigned to a file. For example, the name of a Web page file might be *index.html* or *index.htm.*

File Transfer Protocol (FTP): an application program for sending or receiving files from one computer to another.

fill-in forms: components of Web pages that allow you to type in information and submit it to the individual or organization sponsoring the Web site.

flame: use unnecessarily hostile language on the Internet.

folder: organizational structure on a Macintosh computer that may contain files. See *directory.*

FTP: See *File Transfer Protocol.*

FYI: for your information, an abbreviation commonly used in e-mail.

GIF: See *Graphics Interchange Format.*

gigabyte: 1,024 megabytes.

Gopher: menu-based system for exploring resources on the Internet, now seldom used as a result of the popularity of the World Wide Web.

Graphics Interchange Format (GIF): type of image file used in Web pages. Names of files of this type end with the extension *.gif.*

hard drive: storage mechanism on a computer; usually named *c:* on computers running an operating system such as DOS or Microsoft Windows.

header: top part of an e-mail message, which includes at least *To, From, Date,* and *Subject* (as distinguished from the *body*).

hit: (a) visit to a Web page (e.g., "This page has received 5,000 hits this month"); (b) each reference in the list of results obtained from a Web search by a search directory or search engine (e.g., "Your search has yielded 157 hits").

home page: (a) Web page that serves as the principal or main page of a Web site; (b) the first page that appears when a Web browser is opened.

HTML: See *Hypertext Markup Language.*

HTTP: See *Hypertext Transport Protocol.*

hypertext: nonlinear, multilayered system of information in which files (of text, graphics, or audiovisual elements) are linked to each other and are accessed by pointing to or choosing particular references; also called *hypermedia.*

Hypertext Markup Language (HTML): language used for telling a World Wide Web browser how to lay out text (and other media) and how to make links to other parts of a document or other documents.

Hypertext Transport Protocol (HTTP): protocol on which the World Wide Web is based.

icon: picture on a computer screen representing an application or file (e.g., the picture that represents "My Computer" on a computer running Windows 95 or 98).

image map: image composed of several areas, each functioning as a separate link.

IMHO: in my humble opinion, an abbreviation frequently used in e-mail.

image slicing: act of cutting up an image into pieces, which is useful for creating certain visual effects in Web pages.

InterChange: See *Daedalus InterChange.*

internal link: link on a Web page that connects to another Web page stored on the user's local system.

Internet: largest worldwide network of computer networks.

Internet Explorer: popular Web browser produced by Microsoft.

Internet Protocol (IP): protocol that allows a packet of data to traverse multiple networks of computers on its way to its final destination.

Internet Relay Chat (IRC): chat system that enables synchronous discussion.

Internet service provider (ISP): company that provides Internet access.

IP: See *Internet Protocol.*

IRC: See *Internet Relay Chat.*

ISP: See *Internet service provider.*

JavaScript: client-side programming language, developed by Netscape Communications Corp., that is used to add interactive effects to a Web page, such as button rollovers. Note that JavaScript is not the same as the Java programming language.

Joint Photographic Experts Group (JPEG): file format used in Web pages, most commonly for photographs. Names of files in this format have the extension *.jpg* or *.jpeg.*

JPG, JPEG: See *Joint Photographic Experts Group.*

keypals: computer pen pals.

kilobyte: 1,024 bytes.

LAN: See *local-area network.*

Linux: a computer operating system.

Listproc: widely used software used for managing e-mail discussion lists.

Listserv: widely used software used for managing e-mail discussion lists; often used generically to refer to an e-mail discussion list.

load time: time it takes for a Web page to be completely displayed on a monitor screen.

local-area network (LAN): computers in a single location that are connected.

login: user name used to access an account on the Internet. The verb is *log in,* meaning to enter an account by typing the login.

log out: finish, end, or quit using a program. For example, after finishing with e-mail, you log out so no one else can access your account.

lurk: read messages on an on-line discussion list without sending messages to the list.

Mac: abbreviation for Macintosh computer.

Majordomo: software used for managing e-mail discussion lists.

megabyte: 1,048,576 bytes; sometimes abbreviated as *meg* or *MB.*

modem: device that connects a computer to a telephone line. An internal modem comes on a card that fits on a slot inside the computer; an external modem is placed outside.

MOOs: technically, *MUD, object oriented;* a graphic- or text-based multiuser environment where people from around the world can chat in real time and perform a variety of simulations.

MUD: multiuser domain; a text-based computer environment where people can communicate in real time and carry out various types of simulations; for the most part superseded by *MOOs.*

the net: used to refer to the Internet or sometimes to any computer network (e.g., "See you on the net"); sometimes capitalized when referring specifically to the Internet (e.g., "the Net").

netiquette: net etiquette; conventions for polite and appropriate communication on computer networks.

Netizen: a citizen of the Internet. If the Net is viewed as a country, the Netizens are its people.

Netscape Navigator: popular browser used for accessing information on the World Wide Web; a component of the Internet suite Netscape Communicator, which also contains Web page creation software called Composer.

newbie: new Internet user.

newsgroup: discussion group on Usenet.

nomail: option on e-mail lists whereby no messages are sent to your mailbox but you retain list membership and privileges (e.g., sending messages, accessing archives).

off-line browsing: act of viewing Web pages without a live connection to the Internet; possible through the use of off-line browsing software, such as Teleport Pro.

operating system: main software on a computer that runs the other software. Examples are Microsoft Windows 98 and the Macintosh Operating System.

password: secret combination of letters, numbers, or symbols that a person uses to log in to an account, such as an e-mail account or a dial-up Internet account.

PC: personal computer; often refers to a computer running an operating system such as DOS or Microsoft Windows as opposed to a Macintosh computer.

Point-to-Point Protocol (PPP): protocol that allows a computer with a modem and telephone line to provide a maximum Internet connection.

portal: Web site that serves as an entry site to the World Wide Web and that includes many links to resources (e.g., *Netscape Netcenter*).

post: send a message to a discussion list or newsgroup.

PPP: See *Point-to-Point Protocol.*

protocol: format for transmitting data between computers.

QuickTime: Apple Computer's standard video and animation technology.

QuickTime VR: version of Apple Computer's QuickTime software that lets you rotate images in three dimensions.

real-time communication: communication that takes place immediately, with all participants simultaneously logged on to their computers and messages being transferred instantaneously; also called *synchronous communication.*

relative link: hyperlink that connects to a file stored on the local system; also called *local link.* See also *absolute link.*

right-click: act of clicking the right mouse button.

ring: See Web ring.

robot: automated program that acts as an agent for another program. The most common are *spiders*, which search the Internet for files or information.

schMOOze University: MOO for English language learners and teachers (based in part on a cow motif). See *MOO.*

search engine: program that searches a database for specific key words and returns results displayed on the screen. Typically, search engines (e.g., *Google*) compile information from spiders (Web robots that catalogue public Web information).

search index: search tool that is organized for browsing by headings and subheadings (e.g., *Yahoo!*); similar to a search engine but compiled and organized by people. A search index may also contain a search feature that enables you to scan the database by key word.

Serial Line Internet Protocol (SLIP): protocol that allows a computer with a modem and telephone line to provide a maximum Internet connection.

server: (a) software that allows a computer to offer a service to another computer (the other computers contact the server software by using a matching client software); (b) computer on which the server software runs.

signature: short file often inserted at the end of e-mail messages that includes the sender's name, e-mail address, or other information. Most e-mail software allows you to create a signature file and have it automatically inserted in all messages.

site license: license to use computer software on a large number of computers, such as those in a computer laboratory.

SLIP: See *Serial Line Internet Protocol.*

snail mail: mail delivered by the postal service.

spam: unwanted, unsolicited e-mail, such as commercial advertisements, sent out to groups of people; also a verb meaning to send such e-mail.

spider: program that scans the Web to compile information into a database that is part of an on-line search tool.

streaming audio and video files: files whose contents are transferred from their source to your computer in a steady, continuous fashion and are played as they arrive.

surf the Net: use various tools to look for information on the Internet.

synchronous communication: communication that takes place immediately, with all participants simultaneously logged on to their computers and messages being transferred instantaneously; also called *real-time communication.*

Telnet: software that allows you to log on to a remote computer.

TESL-L: popular e-mail discussion list for English language teachers.

thread: strand of discussion taking place on a discussion board or in a computer conference.

thumbnail: small image that, when clicked on, takes you to a larger image.

under construction: expression used by some Web page creators to indicate that their Web site is not yet finished.

Universal Resource Locator or Uniform Resource Locator (URL): address system used on the World Wide Web for finding resources throughout the Internet (e.g., the URL of the international organization TESOL is http:// www.tesol.org).

UNIX: computer operating system used on many of the mainframe computers that help operate the Internet.

upload: copy computer files in a direction away from you (e.g., from your personal computer into your Internet directory; from your Internet directory to a remote computer).

URL: See *Universal Resource Locator.*

Usenet: informal collection of more than 5,000 newsgroups that exchange news and information.

userid: user identification; the name or nickname a person chooses for a login and e-mail address. The userid is the part of the e-mail address before the @ sign (e.g., *president* in president@whitehouse.gov).

virtual: conceptual; having no physical reality; often used to describe something that is on-line, such as an on-line storefront.

virus: harmful programming code that enters a computer from a file that originates outside the computer.

WAN: See *wide-area network.*

the Web: See *World Wide Web.*

Webmaster: person who creates and maintains a Web site.

Web page: text file stored on a Web server that contains a unique Internet address.

Web ring: group of Web sites that agree to link together in a circular fashion, with each Web site containing a link to the next site in the ring somewhere on its home page (e.g., *ESLoop*).

Web server: computer that permits users on the Internet to access files.

Web site: series of Web pages connected by links.

what you see is what you get (WYSIWYG): characterization of software that allows you to see on the screen exactly what you type on the keyboard.

wide-area network (WAN): computers that are networked together over a broad geographical area.

window: rectangular area on your screen; part of a graphical user interface or graphical operating system, like Windows 98 or Macintosh Operating System.

Windows: popular computer operating system developed by Microsoft.

World Wide Web: all-in-one, hypertext-based system for accessing various resources on the Internet. Also referred to as *the Web* or *WWW.*

World Wide Web Consortium (W3C): international, vendor-neutral organization, founded in 1994, that is devoted to developing common Internet protocols and standards.

worm: computer virus that attaches itself to an e-mail message and automatically sends the message and virus to multiple e-mail addresses

WWW: See *World Wide Web.*

WYSIWYG: See *what you see is what you get.*

XML: See *Extensible Markup Language.*

zip disk: data storage mechanism that is similar to a diskette in function but that can store at least 100 megabytes of information.

zip drive: device that allows you to use zip disks for the storage of information.

Also Available From TESOL

CALL Environments:
Research, Practice, and Critical Issues
Joy Egbert and Elizabeth Hanson-Smith, Editors

E-Mail for English Teaching:
Bringing the Internet and Computer Learning Networks
Into the Language Classroom
Mark Warschauer

New Ways in Content-Based Instruction
Donna M. Brinton and Peter Master, Editors

New Ways in English for Specific Purposes
Peter Master and Donna M. Brinton, Editors

New Ways in Teaching Adults
Marilyn Lewis, Editor

New Ways in Teaching English at the Secondary Level
Deborah J. Short, Editor

New Ways in Using Authentic Materials in the Classroom
Ruth E. Larimer and Leigh Schleicher, Editors

New Ways in Using Communicative Games in Language Teaching
Nikhat Shameem and Makhan Tickoo, Editors

New Ways of Classroom Assessment
James Dean Brown, Editor

New Ways of Using Computers in Language Teaching
Tim Boswood, Editor

Teacher Education
Karen E. Johnson, Editor

Teaching in Action: Case Studies From Second Language Classrooms
Jack C. Richards, Editor

Technology-Enhanced Learning Environments
Elizabeth Hanson-Smith, Editor

For more information, contact
Teachers of English to Speakers of Other Languages, Inc.
700 South Washington Street, Suite 200
Alexandria, Virginia 22314 USA
Tel. 703-836-0774 • Fax 703-836-6447 • publications@tesol.org •
http://www.tesol.org/

Founded 1966